The Eye
of the Storm

THE EYE OF THE STORM

A People's Politics for the Seventies

ALBERT GORE

HERDER AND HERDER

1970
HERDER AND HERDER NEW YORK
232 Madison Avenue, New York 10016

Library of Congress Catalog Card Number: 78–110076

Manufactured in the United States

Contents

DEDICATION

This book is dedicated to the love and loyalty that ever prevails in my family: to my wife, Pauline; to our daughter, Nancy; our son, Albert A. Gore, Jr.; our daughter-in-law, Mary Elizabeth; and our son-in-law, Frank Hunger. Their encouragement and assistance make public service a joy and made this writing pleasurable.

Introduction

In the pages that follow, I have written mainly about political practice rather than about political theory. This does not imply disdain for the theoretical—quite the opposite. Yet the worth of theory can be tested only in the context of practical political action.

I write, too, about those political deeds, forces, and events with which I have been personally involved, both because I know more about them, and also because it is in the issues having the greatest importance for the years ahead that I have intentionally concentrated my political efforts. Since tomorrow grows out of today, I have sought to deal with recent legislative, diplomatic, political, and military history as it relates to the future.

This book, then, is neither encyclopedic in scope, nor primarily a theoretical treatise. It is the testimony of an active politician who seeks the practical application of principles. The principles that I have pursued, the policies that I have espoused, are now the center of a raging political storm, which not only engulfs Tennessee, but has a national bearing, because unless peace and the progressive principles for a people's government prevail at the state level, then they lose at the national level. That is the reason for this book.

One of the tragic events of our history, one that is crucial to the past and present, and one which casts a dark shadow over the future, has been our involvement in war in Southeast Asia, an involvement which has disrupted and threatens further to frustrate our country's historic goals. I therefore begin this book with a discussion of the war in Vietnam, and I try to convey some of the contradictory policies, the paradoxic reversals, the erratic shifts of strategy, the misconstructions and deceptions, in a form of narrative which does not move in strict chronological order, but which shifts back and forth across the time sequence, across the causes, the actions, and the participants, in order to convey by a kind of verbal montage the whole preposterous, indeed hallucinatory, social, political, and military scene. In the next chapter I take up the questions of our foreign policy, followed by an examination of some of the less dramatic—but nevertheless essential—programs we must invest in for the future: social and economic justice, use of resources, election reform, Congressional ethics, etc., and I conclude with a treatment of the maintenance of order in our present-day society, an order that has been violently disrupted as the consequence of our tragic Southeast Asian adventure. The book is thus bracketed, as are our entire politics, or rather, our entire lives, by that disastrous war in Indo-China.

I am very grateful for the assistance of Mrs. Christine Coe, formerly the Washington Editor of *McCall's* magazine, and a longtime personal friend; Jack Lynch, an able veteran of my staff; and William Allen, my Administrative Assistant.

The Eye of the Storm

1.

Vietnam and National Priorities

In February, 1970, a young man from Tennessee was killed in Vietnam, another casualty in a war which some have come to accept almost casually. There was nothing about his death to distinguish it from thousands of others except that just a few days before it occurred this nineteen-year-old soldier had sent his family a letter with a request that it be opened and read at his funeral if he were killed. In that letter he denounced the futility of the war and the "uselessness" of his own death. And, indeed, it did seem useless: at nineteen to have one's life arbitrarily snatched away for a cause which its leaders could not carry out, which its defenders could not justify, and which the world could not approve.

But will history regard this death as useless and ineffectual? Rather, will it not be said, and rightly so, that in this voice from beyond the grave the silent majority of Americans found their most eloquent spokesman? For this was not the voice of one who disdained his country, its institutions, or its flag. It was the voice of one selflessly crying out in witness, not for his own safety, but for the safety of his friends and comrades still living who might be destined to a similar fate.

Perhaps the only real silent majority are the dead and the hundreds of thousands of wounded and maimed whose mute testimony we are too calloused, too hardhearted to listen to.

For me personally, there is bitter irony as well as dismal tragedy in the fact that during our first sixteen years in South Vietnam we made decisions which could lead only and inevitably to the one thing no reasonable American wanted: a bloody Asiatic war with moral and political paralysis at home—an American nightmare come true. I say the *first* sixteen years because so far, by mid-1970, I can glimpse in the definable future neither the will nor the policies nor the actions to extricate us from this quagmire. Of course, one must always hope—but one should not confuse hopes with reality.

In pursuit of a mission undertaken rather modestly in 1954, and escalated until mid-1968, for the stated high purpose of restoring stability and unity to a war-wracked and divided little country—so that its people might choose their own form of government in free elections—we have lost friends around the world, have sent more than two million young Americans to participate in what has been accurately defined as "the wrong war at the wrong place at the wrong time," and in the end, have influenced the Vietnamese only to fight each other and *us* all the more fanatically. This destruction and suffering have left a lasting legacy of hatred.

Allegedly seeking civilian solutions, but allowing the decisions to be made predominantly by the military, we found ourselves propelled into an undeclared war which became increasingly more violent and insoluble. Paradoxically, the more heavily we escalated, the more inextricably we were bogged down. The more we sought a military solution in Vietnam, the more we suffered from political division at home. We could have destroyed North Vietnam, certainly, at any time; but that was never the objective and the price of so doing, possibly war with China, was intolerable. The next major escalation, many warned and a few may have hoped, would have been to nuclear weapons. Fortunately we were not that demented. So a war which, on the only terms available to us, our government neither sought nor could afford to win, became a war of pacification which failed to pacify.

In the meantime, the civil war among the Vietnamese was being enlarged. We were allied to one side, a South Vietnamese military junta, which as the years passed represented fewer and fewer of the South Vietnamese people. And so we ended up fighting the North Vietnamese less than we fought the Viet Cong—not particularly because the latter were South Vietnamese, but merely because they dared oppose the regime we had sponsored and because they were aligned with the "Communists."

As the Viet Cong increased their number so did we increase our aid, our men, and our fire power. The destruction of lives, properties, and values in South Vietnam was devastating. Village after village was destroyed, the leaders killed, the people uprooted, their possessions scattered. The number of refugees grew uncountably, and there was no safe place for them to flee. South Vietnam, regarded more and more by the United States as a separate nation, had already received 900,000 refugees from the North after Vietnam was divided in 1954. It seemed at times as though the whole population was on the move in all directions, seeking safety behind battle lines which failed to stabilize. In this guerrilla war which ravaged the entire land, no man's home was safe against destruction.

It became increasingly clear that our march to war was motivated more by dislike of Communism than by devotion to democracy. One of the most appalling consequences of the war has been that through it we inadvertantly fostered Communist imperialism rather than hampered it. We did this by providing the two Communist giants, China and Russia, with a common cause against Western intervention in Asia. This provided a powerful basis on which they could agree, and thus encouraged—though apparently to no avail, happily for us—a healing of the breach between them. I remarked in a closed session of the Senate Foreign Relations Committee in January of 1966, "the equation between the three great powers, the United States, Russia, and China, seems to me the most important thing involved here."

As to democratic processes in Vietnam and our national hesitation to abide by them, it has been my belief that our own welfare could not be jeopardized by the outcome of any election in which both North and South Vietnam participated, nor in fact by any other political development in Vietnam.

When we went into Vietnam in 1954, we did so following the conference at which the Geneva Accords were settled and by which we tacitly agreed to abide. President Eisenhower decided to send aid and advisors to South Vietnam, partly, I believe, in response to anti-Communist political pressure from within the United States—which was great—and partly in homage to the military nostrum of the day, the "domino theory." He made it clear, though, that no combat troops would be sent to the area, and that our sole aim was to help the South Vietnamese help themselves.

Those Accords, whether we wish to recall them or not, plainly called for an election under international supervision "in July, 1956," in which both North and South Vietnam would participate, and in which the unification of North and South Vietnam would be determined. That election is still called for, and no number of plebiscites in South Vietnam can erase it or ultimately obviate the question of unification. Perhaps President Eisenhower and Secretary Dulles were hopeful that at the end of two years South Vietnam would be a viable democracy and that the results of an open election would constitute a political victory for the United States. However, that was never even remotely probable either in 1954 or in 1956—and it is not in prospect today.

The policy we have been pursuing, therefore, can properly be called neither enlightened self-interest nor unenlightened self-interest. It is plainly unenlightened self-disinterest: that is, political and moral folly. I believe the passage of time and the dismal course of events, including those occurring most recently during the Nixon Administration, have vindicated this judgment.

Recalling the admonition of President Franklin Roosevelt about involving ourselves in the affairs of European colonial empires, I was opposed to our sending U.S. troops to aid the French at Dien Bien Phu, and though a freshman Senator, I voiced that opposition to Senate leaders and others. Subsequently, time after time in the Senate Foreign Relations Committee, I questioned our purposes and raised objections to our policy—questions and objections which in many cases have not been made public until the present writing.

Thus when talks were scheduled to begin (according to the terms of the Geneva Accords) for the preparation of all-Vietnam elections in July, 1956, I was shocked at the South's rejection of the North's invitation merely to discuss them. This intransigence about even *discussing* plans for the elections was particularly disturbing since—it had been agreed at Geneva—such elections were to be held under international supervision. The response of the South Vietnamese government displayed its unwillingness to comply with the Geneva Accords (one of many such displays), and also indicated that the government of South Vietnam had no intention of agreeing to reunification. Such a situation, I maintained, would make of South Vietnam a South Korea-like dependency, extending the need for U.S. aid endlessly into the future. But of course I did not foresee that we would be enmeshed in a major war as a consequence.

I had reported, after a visit to Vietnam in 1958, that a taint of corruption and waste hung over Saigon, that the Strategic Hamlet Program, the pacification model of that time, was impractical, wasteful, and doomed to failure—which it surely was. In 1960, North Vietnam protested several times to the International Control Commission against an increase of personnel in the American Military Assistance and Advisory Group in South Vietnam. This struck me as singularly ominous, especially when it was followed by a U.S. announcement that the Group would be doubled in size from 327 to 685 members; but I expressed my doubts about the purpose of our actions only inside the Committee, on the ground that we were engaged in a wide-spread cold war, economically and politically, with the forces of the Soviet. This was in 1960. There were many other critical areas in the world, and I sincerely wished to agree with President Eisenhower when he envisioned the struggle ahead as a hopeful one.

After the inauguration of my friend, John F. Kennedy, I personally conveyed to him—several times—my deepening concern about our involvement in Vietnam. President

Eisenhower had left him with a heavy burden to carry, especially in the acute situation in Laos, which General Eisenhower called the key to the entire area of Southeast Asia, and I wanted to help the new President in whatever way possible.

The more our aid was increased, the more urgent was my recommendation that we avoid further entanglement. My advice became frequent and insistent within the sessions of the Senate Foreign Relations Committee. In October, 1963, at a closed Committee hearing I told Secretary McNamara:

> "I certainly can lay no claim to being an expert on the situation in Vietnam. I spent no more time there than you. I am certainly not a military man. I have had no more training in that regard than you have, but I must say that as a layman, I have questioned the enormous importance which the military attaches to South Vietnam.
>
> "I know of no strategic material that it has, I know of nothing in surplus supply there except poor people and rice. It seems to me we have no need for either.
>
> "Why must we suffer such great losses in money and lives for an area which seems to me unessential to our welfare, and to freedom, there being none there. . . ?"

And in the following month during another executive Committee hearing I told Secretary Rusk and others:

> "I cannot speak too strongly my deep feelings that this constant and repetitive identity of the United States with military coups and repressive regimes will in the long run erode the image of the United States in many parts of the world. I have thought for three years we should find a way to withdraw our support from them. I am not sure we are not worse off now than we were before we supported them."

But because I did not want, even unintentionally, to obstruct any efforts towards a peaceful resolution on the part of the Executive and because I hadn't yet completely clarified to my satisfaction my own course on this ambiguous issue, I continued to remain silent on the floor of the Senate. I now see that this was a mistake. Although there are few political matters on which one can have absolute certainty, one ought, however, to speak out publicly when possessed of a deep conviction on certain crucial problems and issues, even where complete clarity is unattainable—provided one does so after serious and conscientious reflection. The office of Senator is not merely legislative; it is also informative. And the Senate floor and Senate Committee hearings pro-provide the most effective public forum for this educative function.

Also, and here the whole Congress was grievously remiss, I erroneously voted for the Tonkin Gulf Resolution in 1964. I did so, let it be said, upon the representation that our ships had suffered an "unprovoked attack" in international waters. Later I discovered, and took a leading role in revealing, that the events on that dark, murky, and fateful night in Tonkin Gulf provided but fragile, if any, justification for our subsequent action. *Had* U.S. vessels suffered, or should they now suffer, an "unprovoked attack" in international waters, "an appropriate but limited response" *would* appear justified, and I would again so vote. It never occurred to me that such flimsy facts as were later revealed, if indeed they were facts, would be used as either a reason or a pretext for a major military onslaught. (Whether President Johnson himself was misinformed and thus misled, I do not know but hope some day to learn.)

This Resolution, it turned out, was the prop Johnson felt he needed from Congress to support him in his initial bombing attack on North Vietnam, and which he later claimed supported all the other military actions taken during his administration. Later, I saw him pull a copy of the Resolution out of his inside coat pocket and brandish it about as though it were some sort of license to do as he pleased. The State Department interpreted it officially as the "functional equivalent" of a declaration of war. Many Senators denied the validity of this interpretation, and I am sure this was not the legislative intent of the Senate.

It would be otiose to question whether without the Tonkin Gulf Resolution President Johnson might have claimed some other ground to justify escalating the conflict; the point I am making here is that when I discovered that the Congress had been misled I soon took steps to correct it. I began to raise critical questions about the war—its legality, its morality, its wisdom, and its justification—and to criticize the Tonkin Resolution on the Senate floor and elsewhere. On April 8, 1965, for instance, I declared at an executive session of the Senate Foreign Relations Committee:

> "President Johnson made a very important speech to the world last night. There were many plusses in that speech. He asserted his willingness to seek a negotiated settlement. Those of us who had earlier suggested *that* were pictured as Quislings . . .
>
> "Let me recall to you that we passed a resolution last year after the Tonkin Gulf incident. I did not interpret that resolution as the vesting of any additional power in the Presidency.
>
> "Yet we are told that Congress had already endorsed by that resolution everything that has been done since then, *plus* whatever other action may be taken in the future.
>
> "Now had I had any notion that such interpretation

could or would be placed on it I would have joined the Senator from Oregon and the Senator from Alaska in voting against it."

I shall continue to criticize this Johnsonian interpretation of the Tonkin Gulf Resolution—an interpretation which Vice-President Spiro Agnew during his tour of Vietnam publicly embraced,. presumably at the behest of the Nixon Administration—though the Administration later interposed no objection to its repeal, saying that it did not rely upon it for authority to act in Southeast Asia or elsewhere. I voted for its repeal, being guided here as elsewhere by the conviction that the views I express and the votes I cast arise out of the responsibility given to me in stewardship by the voters of Tennessee; a responsibility to protect the interests of the people of my state and of my country. Those two interests are one and the same, are indissoluble, on Vietnam, as on virtually every other issue.

In our differences over Vietnam, we have let ourselves become hypnotized into self-delusion. We have gradually accepted the unholy, autistic reality that war creates. We have let Vietnam become a matter of partisan politics; and frequently we have devalued our moral currency to compound political nostrums and cater to prejudices, resorting to crude face-saving devices which counterfeit our highest traditional value and violate our rightful pride in being the world's greatest democracy. We must de-mesmerize ourselves, break through the shell of public relation formulae and jingoist slogans, and dispassionately analyze the kernel of our national interest. What we must really be concerned about is saving the soul of our country and our individual honor and conscience.

Four American Presidents have tried to cope with the

issue of Vietnam, and two of them were elected because they seemed at the time to be the best hope of terminating our presence there on an honorable basis. The first of these was Lyndon Johnson in 1964 in a contest with super-hawk Barry Goldwater whose campaign tract, *A Fresh Look at American Foreign Policy,* staled rapidly when adopted by Johnson himself immediately after the election. The second is Richard Nixon who openly admits that his election carried with it a clear "mandate from the American people" to end the war in Vietnam. As I see it, there has been no "silent majority" quietly egging the warriors on to greater heights up the escalation ladder and urging that the carnage be prolonged. The people have spoken openly and definitely against the war in *two* national elections.

Secretary Dulles could not bring himself to face up to an election in Vietnam which our intelligence reports indicated would surely go in favor of Ho Chi Minh. He therefore never sought to implement the election agreed upon in the Geneva Accords. The "military-industrial complex," about which President Eisenhower would later warn the nation, opposed holding the election. I distinctly remember hearing General Maxwell Taylor saying in a jocular aside: "We are for self-determination if they determine *our* way."

With the election of President Nixon the country came full circle back to Eisenhower's Vice-President. In his first speech on Vietnam to the American people on May 14, 1969, the new President indicated that he had apparently become a wiser man—just as his press agents proclaimed. In his program for ending the war he seemed to say that he, too, had come full circle back to the Geneva Accords.

I applauded this speech and took heart from it, not only because the President ruled out a "purely military solution on the battlefield"—which seemed to me to leave a peaceful settlement or compromise as the only viable alternative

—but also because in his plans for a settlement he advanced a number of steps which I had long advocated: first, creation of an international body agreeable to both sides to supervise troop withdrawals and cease fires; second, "all parties would agree to observe the Geneva Accords of 1954 regarding South Vietnam and Cambodia, and the Laos Accords of 1962"; third, "mutual withdrawal of non-South Vietnamese forces from South Vietnam and free choice for the people of South Vietnam." In support of this latter point the President condemned, in three different places in his speech, "a one-sided withdrawal"—a fact of considerable importance which I shall take up later. And he went on to say: "Almost without exception the leaders of non-Communist Asia have told me that they would consider a one-sided American withdrawal from Vietnam to be a threat to the security of their own nations."

He did not rule out a coalition government. It had been my view for a long while that a compromise government and neutrality status for the former French colonies was the most feasible form of settlement in consonance with the terms of the Geneva Accords. In fact, the President said: "We have no objection to reunification, if that turns out to be what the people of North Vietnam and the people of South Vietnam want; we ask only that the decision reflect the free choice of the people concerned."

It was my view of the speech that the President had decided to use the mandate of his election, as Eisenhower had with the Korean war, to extricate the United States from Vietnam as quickly as he could, as best he could, and as honorably as he could. For this decision, I congratulated him and wished him the greatest good fortune in a speech on the floor of the Senate. Now, I know for a fact that this benign interpretation of the speech was encouraged by Dr. Henry Kissinger, National Security Affairs Assistant to

President Nixon, in a number of remarks and in telephone calls he made to several Senators on the Foreign Relations Committee.

Secretary of State Rogers was sent to Saigon at the time of the speech to placate the generals there who, unless they had changed their views—and there had been no indication of this—could be expected to be against many of President Nixon's proposals; just as all along they had opposed any genuine Vietnamese peace or any South Vietnamese government but their own. Apparently Secretary Rogers was not very successful, for President Nguyen Van Thieu immediately demanded the meeting with President Nixon which was held three weeks later in June at Midway Island.

Incidentally, I long have thought it was beneath the dignity of a President of the United States to run to summit meetings with the beribboned and bemedalled Thieu-Ky regime every time it blew the whistle. I specifically advised against this particular Nixon-Thieu conference in an executive session of the Foreign Relations Committee on May 28, 1969, saying that it would give Thieu "leverage to which he is not entitled."

Immediately before the Midway summit meeting, Thieu had been making obvious efforts to forestall any prospects of a political settlement which would not guarantee the continuation in power of his junta. He went to South Korea, to Formosa, and to the Philippines soliciting allies and loudly exhorting them not to abandon him as he sought to box President Nixon into abandoning his peace plan. Cacophonous screams of anger emanated from all these capitals against any move to "appease" the Communists. And the self-decorated and self-appointed marshals and generals in Saigon proclaimed that any election held must be "in accordance with the constitution of South Vietnam."

One notes almost comically—if it weren't fraught with tragedy—that the South Vietnamese constitution, which was promulgated by Saigon with support from the United States, makes illegal "every activity designed to propagate or implement Communism," which, coupled with an electoral law that prevents neutralists from running for office, has the effect of limiting candidates to those who do not offend the ruling junta. To call this a "democratic constitution" is simply to indulge in newspeak. Yet that was precisely President Thieu's idea of self-determination. Similarly, administration spokesmen have referred to the South Vietnamese constitution as "an historic document insuring basic human and political rights," and have hailed Thieu's own "election" as a showcase event illustrating how the will of the people had prevailed—even though with firm U.S. support he had received only a small minority of votes cast.

I thought it was time we acknowledged that the Thieu-Ky regime does not represent democracy in any acceptable sense of the term. Like the so-called "guided democracies" of the Soviet empire, the Saigon junta makes a mockery of the right to free speech and freedom of the press, jails political and religious leaders who advocate either neutrality or a coalition of all the people of South Vietnam, and, lastly, subverts the very principles of self-determination and democratic freedom for which the United States professes to be fighting.

We do not have to force a coalition or any other political modality on the South Vietnamese. We have only to define our terms—a compromise based on a coalition regime—and give the Saigon government a simple choice: to join us in negotiating peace on those terms, or to continue the war on its own, for as long as it likes or is able. And in that event we would be free in all honor to make our own peace on terms reflecting the national security requirements of the United States. The association of these requirements with the political ambitions of the Saigon generals is and always has been a mistake. We have only to recognize that mistake to free ourselves for peace.

But as the Midway meeting approached, all the factious fury coming from Thieu and his cohorts was echoed here at home. The hawks screamed about giving in to "the Communists" and President Nixon himself made another speech on June 4 at the Air Force Academy which struck a chord quite different from that of his speech of May 14—and which, in fact, added up to a ringing defense of the military: "It is open season on the armed forces. . . . Patriotism is considered by some to be a backward, unfashionable fetish of the uneducated and unsophisticated. . . . We shall reaffirm our aspiration to greatness or we shall choose instead to withdraw into ourselves. . . ."

Pro-Vietnam elements in the press, Nixon's constant champions, prominently and regularly printed stories and editorials about the dangerous consequences of Communist appeasement. The *Chicago Tribune* of May 16, 1969, editorialized: "When the United States assured a commitment of those dimensions, it could not simply cut and run at a later date without risking the reproach of betraying its allies and forfeiting its responsibilities to the cause of a peaceful and stable world. A disguised defeat would merely encourage the Communists to embark on further adventures on a larger and more dangerous scale."

At Midway, as so frequently before, an American President found himself stymied. Hemmed in by political pressures at home, by a wily "ally" abroad, and by insistent military advice from both places, President Nixon quietly shifted gears and proceeded full-speed—where? Into reverse! Without formally announcing the abandonment of his May 14 peace plan, President Nixon simply charted a different course—"phased withdrawal." The psychological sop he offered the American people was proclamation of a gradual "unilateral withdrawal"—denounced thrice in his speech of only a month before—of 25,000 American troops, with further disengagement promised for the future. In a phrase worthy of coinage by his Vice-President's ghost writers (shall we call it "Agnewspeak?"), President Nixon launched his scheme with the Madison Avenue title: "Vietnamization." For the home market this proved to be an attractive package, at least temporarily; but the contents had yet to be appraised and tested, though they surely were not new.

In fact, Nixon's adopted brainchild, "Vietnamization," resulted from a liaison between the Pentagon and Saigon in the fall of 1968. Before leaving office as Secretary of Defense, Clark Clifford had said in a report: "We will continue to seek ways to effect a reduction of hostilities to lower the level of violence in South Vietnam, and to turn over more and more defense responsibilities to the South Vietnamese themselves."

But regardless of who first engineered this scheme, there is no doubt that it was a far cry from Nixon's earlier "plan" to end the war with a peaceful settlement. Acknowledging that the return home of any soldier is most welcome, I warned in the Senate that a "phased withdrawal" that involved keeping U.S. military forces in South Vietnam to prop up the Saigon military regime until it *could* and *would* maintain itself in power was simply a covert formula for prolonging instead of ending the war.

Furthermore, I suggested that none of the three preconditions for withdrawal from Vietnam was within the control of the United States:

1. *Progress in peace negotiations in Paris.* Without a high-ranking representative there, the conference will be

downgraded. As Theodore H. White wrote at the time, neither side "has offered the other more than impossible and humiliating surrender."

2. *The will and ability of Saigon government to defend itself.* What happens to "Vietnamization" if current optimistic assessments of the stability of the Saigon regime prove as groundless as others?

3. *The level of enemy activity.* It would seem logical that the enemy would like nothing better than to hold the "level" of their activity low in South Vietnam while watching the withdrawal of U.S. forces. It certainly should be less costly to them to count the number of departing U.S. soldiers than to attempt to decimate them by combat.

Moreover, by keeping the "level" of their activities low in South Vietnam, their forces can be shifted to Laos or Cambodia, or be readied for that possible date when an attack on a reduced U.S. force would be more inviting. Yet the Administration asserted that somehow the withdrawal of U.S. troops from South Vietnam, coupled with more equipment and training for the South Vietnamese Army, would put pressure on North Vietnam to negotiate a settlement. The very contrary appears more logical. Indeed, "Vietnamization" and negotiation appear to be absolute incompatibles. "Vietnamization" relies for success upon maintaining the Thieu-Ky regime and its military establishment in power. On the other hand, a policy of negotiation would require the U.S. to persuade a coalescence of forces, factions, and factors in Vietnam into a compromise government which would require that Thieu and Ky step down from the pinnacle of power on which "Vietnamization" proposes to keep them.

I urged a negotiated settlement which I believed, and which I still believe, was then possible—more likely then than now—for a newly-elected President to bring about.

Moreover, I believe this offered the best chance for the ultimate emergence of democratic forces and genuine self-determination in South Vietnam. On the Senate floor, I pleaded:

> "It is my view that we should utilize our overwhelming presence in Vietnam to persuade the establishment of a broadly based government that would include the diverse factors, sects, and factions to serve as a means of concluding a peaceful settlement and to provide some hope for the ultimate survival of democratic processes and freedom in South Vietnam. . . .
>
> "Every American who is returned home from Vietnam gladdens our heart, the more the better. But the peace program that is in the vital interest of the United States and in the interest of world-wide peace, and one which I believe the American people earnestly desire, is one which will lead to a peaceful settlement of the war and one which will permit all U.S. troops, not just a few at a time over a long withdrawal period, to be disengaged and returned to the peaceful and fruitful pursuits of a normal life."

But no argument, however cogent, would avail. A "negotiated settlement" had lost its priority—displaced by the urgency of keeping the Thieu-Ky regime in power in Saigon, and so continuing the war. "Vietnamization" was merely a semantic cover for continuing in South Vietnam a putative Democratic Republic controlled, of course, by people of our approval.

When President Nixon met with Thieu at Midway he may have learned something new—new to him at least—about Thieu-ism: a capacity to say one thing one day and the opposite the next day without appearing to know the difference. At any rate, the President of the United States smoothed Thieu's ruffled feathers, called him a great political leader, and—most ironic of all—praised him for agreeing to hold internationally supervised elections. President Nixon then pledged that "We will accept the result of those elections and the South Vietnamese will as well, even if it is a Communist government." There can be no doubt that Thieu had assured the President on this point; otherwise, the statement could not have been made.

But the very next day, Thieu was declaring that his country "will not stop short of victory, no matter what happens in Washington." He defined victory as "no Communist domination and no coalition with the Communists." Emboldened by his return to his own capital, he asserted: "There will be no coalition government, no peace cabinet, no transitional government, not even a reconcilatory government." The next month, all consistency thrown aside, President Nixon himself flew to Vietnam and there, standing beside President Thieu, referred to the U.S. role in the Vietnam war as "*perhaps our finest hour*." And, what of Mr. Thieu? Reporters aboard Airforce One wrote that in a conversation with them in flight from Saigon the President had called Thieu one of the four or five best politicians in the world. In sociological jargon this is known as "winning the acceptance of one's peer group." As I observed on the floor of the Senate, April 16, 1970:

> "Whatever General Thieu's position may lack in wisdom or concern for the Vietnamese people, it is more than made up for in clarity and forthrightness. But where does Thieu get the power to make it stick? From the minority of the South Vietnamese people who support his rule? From the dispirited Army of the Republic of Vietnam with its military strategy of "search and avoid"? Where then does this small-time dictator get the power to dominate events, while America's vast resources crumble like clay in the hands of

its statesmen? The answer lies in the astonishing subservience of the American government to the Saigon generals."

Soon after the President's return to the White House from Midway, a number of visitors quoted him as saying that he would not be the first President to negotiate a U.S. defeat. No one had suggested "defeat" for the U.S., for no responsible person had advocated a chaotic, precipitate withdrawal. And President Nixon himself had taken the war out of the rhetorical context of "victory" or "defeat" in his speech of May 14 by saying that he had ruled out a purely military solution on the battlefield. So it was very discouraging that such an expression of such an attitude in such language would come from the President.

Meanwhile, the further announcement of incremental withdrawals of U.S. troops, even though small in number, won widespread popularity. Who could fail to be pleased with the return of American soldiers from the Vietnamese Hamburger Hills? Even leading Democrats—Hubert Humphrey, for instance—praised "Vietnamization," though we had neither been informed what the plan really was nor given any idea whatsoever as to its schedule. And Senator Mike Mansfield, Senate Democratic Leader, called it "a step in the right direction."

U.S. public opinion responded enthusiastically to the appealing promise of "bringing the boys home" *and* of thwarting Communism at the same time. Strangely, even the win-the-war-at-any-price advocates endorsed it. Questions as to whether it was a carefully considered strategy for peace, or a political maneuver to placate the public while continuing the war, seemed off-key. All those asking such "impudent" questions came under the lash of Vice-President

Agnew, who suggested that Americans should "divide on authentic lines."

We were, tragically, traveling once again on the long-war road.

But the *complete* about-face from Nixon's position of May 14 was not publicly accomplished by his June 9 message; it was fully effected only by his television speech to the nation on November 3, 1969. Here he reiterated all the discredited arguments for American involvement in Vietnam, and then affirmed again that he was going to "get us out" of it anyway. But even assuming that "Vietnamization" may get us out of the war *some day*—and it is far from certain that it will, as I have shown—it is extremely difficult to understand *why* Mr. Nixon, believing as he says he does in the wisdom and justice of this war, would still rather withdraw from it than win it. This is a war, he says, for the defense of freedom, for the prevention of world conquest by Communist powers, and for proving America's loyalty to commitments, etc. It is so much in our self-interest that Mr. Nixon is going to withdraw from it!

It was in this same speech that he made his touching plea that the "silent majority" should support his self-contradictory conduct. I am filled with revulsion at the thought of a "silent majority," nor do I think it really exists. The President uses the phrase to flatter complacency, and promote the fantasy of a "Gary Cooper America"—short on words and ideas but strong on guts. What the phrase really identifies is an American denied any real means of participation in specific issues, an American given—and hopefully satisfied with—lulling reassurance instead of hard facts and logic.

Some of the President's foreign-policy advisors counselled against the Johnsonian hard-line language of that speech. But Mr. Nixon insisted, I am reliably informed, that three

American Presidents had sent American boys to their deaths in the jungles of Southeast Asia, and he could not afford to tell the nation that these sacrifices had been in vain. He said, I am most reliably informed, that he must bring "political cohesion" to the country. If one narrowly interprets the President's decision, his language, and his actions, one might conclude that domestic political considerations were an important ingredient, if not the essential one, for this desired "political cohesion." Viewed more broadly, one could conclude that President Nixon thus sought national unity, or at least majority support, for the war at the very price of continuing it.

In either case, the President had passed up his best opportunity to bring the war to a close through a negotiated settlement—and thus had rejected not only his own earlier proposals, but also the mandate of his election. As a result of it all, the peace talks were downgraded by the withdrawal of Ambassador Lodge from Paris, and untold thousands of our young men were doomed to be casualties through the continuation of a war which had been only verbally but not actually de-escalated to any significant extent.

But both verbal and actual de-escalation were the victims of our invasion of Cambodia, perhaps the most bizarre of the mistakes we made in Southeast Asia in 1970. The result of this invasion of a sovereign state was a visible increase in our casualties merely to destroy a few arms caches which, no one can doubt, will be replaced readily enough by the Viet Cong and its allies. The invasion of Cambodia was the subject of a conference between President Nixon and about 50 Senators and Congressmen, members of the Senate Foreign Relations Committee and the House Foreign Affairs Committee, on May 2, 1970, three days after the President had announced ground "attacks" on Cambodia in a dramatic TV address. This had caused a severely critical public outcry over the widening of the war. The Senate Foreign Relations Committee had formally requested a meeting with the President. Instead, the President had invited both the Senate committee and the 35 members of the House committee.

On April 20 the President had made a placatory speech in prime time on three networks in which he had spoken with "confidence" that ". . . we finally have in sight the just peace. . . ." Only ten nights later he had told the same people over the same networks that our situation was so precarious that he had widened the war by ordering ground "attacks" in Cambodia. In this context, there was a recognizable and perhaps understandable tenseness about the meeting, which I want to discuss in some detail because it illustrates fully the arbitrariness of the President's position.

The contrast between the two Presidential TV addresses, only ten nights apart, was more than the country could take with equanimity, the contradiction impossible to reconcile. The President's exposition of his position appeared to me no less muddled and contradictory. His only explanation was that the enemy had taken "actions in Cambodia" that had created a "Cambodian crisis," which meant, the President said, that either we must get out now, we must stop the withdrawals he had announced and planned, or "go to the heart of the problem"—the sanctuaries. I wondered just how this situation had changed between April 20 and April 30. The President answered this, at least for me, when he said that the military had wanted "to hit them for years." "This gives Vietnamization a better chance," he said, adding: "It gives time—buying time for ARVN" (South Vietnamese Army).

The President assured concerned legislators that the operation would be limited in both time and extent and that the invasion would not go deeper than "35 kilometers without the approval of Congress," though he did not say the original plans contained such limits.

The first Senator to speak up, according to my notes, was Senator Jacob K. Javits of New York. He propounded a weighty question about the constitutional equation between the Executive and the Legislative branches with respect to war-making powers. The President replied in legalistic terms which I did not take down, but noted to myself that it was not a "strict construction." I did jot down one sentence the President used in his reply to Senator Javits: "We are getting out . . ." All the while he was explaining and defending the deeper and wider involvement which he had ordered.

Senator Fulbright asked if, in the President's view, China would "accept defeat of North Vietnam." The President replied that we are "not attempting defeat upon North Vietnam," and that he was open to settlement "on the basis of present power balance" in South Vietnam. Senator Fulbright inquired, too, if the President thought the strategic arms limitation talks under way in Vienna would be "adversely affected." The President declared that it would not seriously affect the SALT talks, that the Russians and we had a mutual interest in achieving a limitation of armaments, etc. In the course of his reply he said: "We expect the Soviets to protest this just as we protested their invasion of Czechoslovakia." I thought this a disturbing, and to me an unacceptable, analogy.

When my turn came I inquired: "Mr. President, you have told us that you will not invade deeper than 35 kilometers into Cambodia without the approval of Congress. What is the difference in principle between invading 35 kilometers and 50 kilometers? The important event was the crossing of the boundary of a sovereign nation with an invading Army, which you ordered without authority from or even consultation with Congress. Yet you tell us now you will not go beyond 35 kilometers without the approval of Congress. What is the principle and where is the logic?"

The President tersely replied: "Because this is not a sovereign territory. It had become completely dominated by the enemy," and he sharply turned, pointing to another person on the other side of the room. Though I did not think this answered my question at all, and though I wished further to explore the rationale of both the action and the limits, I was not again recognized—which also illustrated that this was not the kind of "consultation" that the Senate Foreign Relations Committee had desired.

There was no doubt, of course, that the incursion would be a "military success." The sanctuaries could be destroyed just as the Port of Haiphong could be closed and as Hanoi could be levelled. In fact, the General upon whom the President called for a report to us on the military operation told us: "We are meeting very little opposition." The question in my mind was whether in the long run it was a wise decision, whether it would be either useful or conclusive towards peace or disengagement—and where it would end.

After the two-hour conference, I concluded that President Nixon was still following the familiar but unfortunate path of seeking "peace" through a "wider war," was "saving lives" by increasing the casualty rate, pursuing a mirage in Vietnam by a policy that was eroding his own as well as our national credibility, and tragically prolonging the war by making negotiations for peace more difficult.

As I noted earlier, Nixon, in glossing over his reversal and proclaiming his new program for South Vietnam, was merely embracing the Johnson-Thieu strategy, as Johnson had embraced the strategic program of Barry Goldwater.

It was as though one were to tell a movie audience which had sat through an exhausting and harrowing film, "Keep your seats, please. We want to run the film through once again." The death of tens of thousands of American boys, and of hundreds of thousands of North and South Vietnamese, seemed to be regarded as though it were some distant drama to be viewed from a safe, remote vantage point by the military and political spectators. But the plot, the "scenario"—to use one of Herman Kahn's favorite expressions—of the drama was basically the same, only the price of admission had been slightly reduced.

The U.S. military budget for Vietnam for fiscal year 1970 was 24.9 billion dollars, or more than 2 billion dollars a month. This represented a reduction of 4 billion dollars from the budget for Vietnam in 1969—so at least we were not, at the moment, continuing to escalate the war budget —or were we? In a sense, we *were*, because this figure of approximately 25 billion dollars was still greater than the annual average outlay for the preceding four years—nearly a half decade of folly during which we have spent over 106 billion, 700 million dollars. But even this latter figure does not represent the outside limits of the cost of this adventure. It does not include the budgets for the first nine years, nor the 2 billion dollars in aid we supplied to the French when they were fighting to preserve their colonial empire, nor the 4.5 billion dollars in economic aid we have given South Vietnam. Future historians will have as hard a time assessing the cost with accuracy as they will in documenting the war's credibility—but they will clearly see the enormity of our expenditures, even when they cannot comprehend the reasons for them.

Each and every bill making appropriations for the war has had my support. I have drawn a clear distinction between support of our troops in Vietnam, on the one hand,

and approval of the policies that got us into a land war in Asia and that have repeatedly widened and escalated that war, on the other hand. For the most part, the fighting men are there not by choice but in duty to their country and by order of military authority. They deserve the best of weapons, munitions, equipment, medical supplies, food—everything they need—to execute their orders with the least possible danger to themselves. Up to 1970, almost every member of the House and Senate shared this feeling. Congress did, in 1969, limit authorization for use of funds to expand the war into Laos and Thailand. Except for this, an invasion of Laos may have already occurred. There is no explanation, really, as to why Congress did not at that time include Cambodia in this prohibition, except that the likelihood of expansion of the war into Cambodia seems not to have then occurred to anyone.

Congress unquestionably has the constitutional power—the power of the purse—to stop the war by withholding appropriations. This would be an unusual, an extreme, use of constitutional powers by the Legislative branch to restrain the actions of the Executive; no less extreme, of course, than the Presidential usurpation of the war-making power in the case of the Cambodian invasion. Would this be wise? More and more Senators are now considering such a course of action. For my part, I have been very reluctant to do so. It would be better, needless to say, if the President could be persuaded to alter his course of actions, thus avoiding a constitutional crisis, a kind of crisis which our Founding Fathers could not have foreseen—more than 2,000,000 men sent into the longest war in our history without a declaration of war or specific approval of the people or their elected representatives.

I profoundly sympathize with these young men who have sacrificed so much, those now in service, or those who may be drafted and who find themselves in a state of uncertainty and travail as the length of the war has reached the mark of a decade and a half, with still no end in sight. From the time these young men, now faced by the draft, were three or four years old they have grown up in a climate of increasing military violence and, as a consequence, of increasing civilian despair. The prospect of endless war does not provide an atmosphere in which young people —subject to an uncertain and sometimes arbitrary draft for service in a war in which many do not believe—can be expected to remain placid, content, and well-disposed to all the institutions of their society. To continue a war where our vital interests are not involved, and when it is honorably possible—as it has surely been to my mind—to negotiate a peaceful settlement, is heartlessness towards the young who in this, as in other wars, have had to suffer for the errors of their elders.

The bitterness, waywardness, and violence which many deplore in some of our young people have in part certainly been rooted in the Vietnam crisis. Two million boys answered their country's call to a war not of their own making, and they have served more heroically than anyone could have anticipated in this, the most protracted war of our history. No other generation of Americans has been called to such a sacrifice, a sacrifice not merely of their lives but of their very intelligence itself, a sacrifice which demanded their possible death in a war which defies understanding.

It defies understanding because the explanation, or rather the rationalization, of our presence in Vietnam has undergone constant change over the years. Perhaps the most formidable-seeming legal argument has been that our SEATO obligations demanded our intervention: a peculiarly perverse argument when one recalls that SEATO did not go into effect until February 19, 1955, that is, months *after* Eisenhower's commitment letter to aid South Vietnam. Yet Secretary of State Dean Rusk in a public inquiry conducted by the Foreign Relations Committee in early 1966 declared we were upholding our SEATO obligations by continuing to prosecute the war in the South.

And how could there not be widespread misunderstanding when the stated objectives of the war change with every political wind and are so often mis-stated, or simply mistaken? Witness, for instance, the hindsight declaration of former President Johnson in a nationally televised broadcast on February 6, 1970. He never had sought victory in Vietnam "in the usual sense," he said. A "victory" acceptable *to him,* he brought out, was the establishment of an "independent South Vietnam"—a goal precisely the opposite of that of the Geneva Accords with their emphasis on an election to unite the North and South. Mr. Johnson made it abundantly clear that such an "independent South Vietnam" would be something created in our own image and governed by our own friends. Now, the former President might not consider this to be "victory in the usual sense," but there is no doubt that North Vietnam and the Viet Cong would certainly consider it to be total defeat in every sense.

How can there not be misunderstanding about the war when the present administration seems now to have reached the point of not even bothering to justify its action by rational argument? Witness, as we already have, the paradox of President Nixon's declaration that he was "ending the war by Vietnamization"—a "plan to bring peace"—when the political realities clearly indicated that peace can only come to this war-ravaged country through negotiation and compromise. His was the kind of self-contradictory "explanation" which may have provoked Senator Aiken's wry observation that the Senate ought to declare we had won the war and then send word to the boys to come home.

In a similar vein shortly after President Nixon had announced his unilateral withdrawal plans and "Vietnamization" of the war, at a chance brief meeting with Henry Kissinger (who was credited with writing much of the President's May 14 speech), and knowing him well and liking him, I jested with him a bit in the course of our conversation by remarking: "You have come up with the most marvelous formula of the ages in Vietnam—winning by pulling out." "A neat trick if we can pull it off," he smilingly replied. Then, more seriously, he went on to say that anyone who knows Vietnam realizes that one cannot be sure of anything . . . that the administration thinks it has a reasonable chance with what it is doing . . . and that they know nothing better to do. . . , etc. A decisive way to put it! I could have reminded him of his book, *The Necessity for Choice,* and told him that precisely what the Nixon administration wasn't doing was *choosing*. Perhaps Professor Kissinger now will author a sequel to his earlier book to be titled, *The Necessity for Dawdling*.

But any sort of levity can only be speedily dissipated by the somber reality of our course in Vietnam. As I have already indicated, my hope was that President Nixon, while still fresh in office and before the frustrations and pressures of the Presidency had overtaken him, would be able to end the war honorably. And indeed his first plan was admirable, but the desire for domestic "political cohesion" (with Johnson it had been "consensus"), and pressure from the Saigon regime apparently diverted him from it.

This Thieu-Ky regime has grown so under our aegis—*our* "Vietnamization," if you will—it is now in a nose-thumbing position and all too ready to denigrate our efforts towards any peaceful solution. Witness the spiffy Marshal Ky having the effrontery to say in February, 1970, that his country had never asked for American troops: "American policy was wrong in the past when the U.S. wanted to pour in troops to win the guerrilla war," he said. "I told them they should modernize and train our army and not send in large amounts of U.S. troops." Now, I remember only too well most of the actions taken in South Vietnam, even before the military junta in 1963 seized control of the government following the assassination of President Ngo Dinh Diem. I did not want the troops to go in at that time either, but to say that they were not wanted by Saigon would be adding current insult to past injury.

Back in 1963, when the cruel Diem government was using tanks, tear gas, clubs, firearms, and barbed wire to suppress the Buddhist uprisings, when Buddhist priests and nurses were immolating themselves in protest, martial law was imposed with the implicit approval of the U.S. advisors. Secretary of State Dean Rusk called the situation "difficult and dangerous," and said we could not promise and did not expect a quick victory, pointing out that the U.S. role in South Vietnam was "limited and supportive." Even then, after seven years of aid and "Vietnamization," 1963 style, we had made no headway towards peace, and the retrogression at that time was obvious.

I went to the White House late one afternoon and, in a long upstairs visit with President Kennedy, pleaded for a quick and total withdrawal of U.S. advisors and military aid, pointing out to him that religious persecution was something with which neither the U.S. nor he, a member of a faith that had suffered persecution, should be contaminated. I went further and said the persecution of the Buddhists offered him a clear way out, a worthy justification for extricating ourselves from what promised to become a quagmire.

He should issue a statement, I suggested, that the U.S. could not permit herself to be associated with tyranny and religious persecution, and was therefore withdrawing her personnel and aid.

Without directly expressing agreement or disagreement with my suggestion, he frankly discussed the situation and revealed his own deep disturbance over developments in Vietnam and about the Saigon political regime in particular. Moreover, he expressed pessimism about the situation developing generally in Southeast Asia. He said our chances of achieving any lasting success were "very slim." I was particularly impressed when he said: "When China has an arsenal of nuclear weapons, Indo-China is in her sphere of influence." The very next day I had a visit from one of my friends, also one of the President's very closest confidants, who had visited with the President at the White House in the evening following my conference with him. Though our common friend did not say he was quoting or repeating the President, nevertheless I considered I had my answer: "After Cuba [Bay of Pigs] and with China going Communist under Truman, no Democratic President can pull out of Vietnam."

Thus, an opportunity to save ourselves from the quicksand in which we were rapidly sinking was lost to political pragmatism. Sadly, domestic political considerations have exerted an inordinate influence on Vietnam policy throughout the administrations of four Presidents.

A much healthier style of political pragmatism was displayed by Senator Richard Russell of Georgia in his 1966 proposal that a poll be taken in the major cities of South Vietnam as to whether U.S. aid was wanted. If the answer were no, he counseled, then "the U.S. should pull out." Senator Russell also told President Johnson, as I have heard repeated many times around the Democratic Senate roundtable, that he would spend whatever it took, fifty million dollars or more, to bring some Vietnamese "so-and-so" to power, with the understanding that he would then invite us to withdraw our troops; and that five million dollars would be waiting for him in a Swiss bank; and that a plane would be prepared to take him there, when necessary. All utterly fantastic? But this is the kind of nightmare war in which the fantastic takes on the appearance of actuality.

It struck some people as fantastic when I made a speech in Miami in late 1964 suggesting a "negotiated settlement" of the war. (So far as I know, and as incredible as it may now seem, this was the first use of that phrase in connection with the Vietnam predicament.) Its use infuriated several people in my audience, and a number walked out in protest. Fortunately, it did reach the media and caused considerable discussion. I made the same suggestion in Washington after Congress reconvened. Again—and this is the other aspect of the fantastic character of which I speak—it was regarded as news of such significance that it was carried on all the networks—and got me a telephone conversation with President Johnson. In that conversation the most pleasant thing the President was disposed to say to me was, "You *looked* good on TV." My statement was clearly displeasing to him, and it may have helped motivate him soon to invite Congressmen and Senators in groups to the White House for briefings on our policy in Vietnam.

At these sessions, the President would lead off and then call on Secretary Rusk, Secretary of Defense McNamara, and various members of the military. All denounced any hint of a negotiated settlement: it would give aid and comfort to the enemy (how often have we heard that?) . . . create devisiveness at home, etc., etc. But then, only a few months later, the theme was picked up by Johnson himself and in his Johns Hopkins University address he publicly advocated a "settlement by negotiation."—My last and final illustration of the paradoxic, fantastic, and hallucinatory nature of the war itself and of those who were directing it.

The complete break between Johnson and myself on South Vietnam came at one of those briefing sessions when we talked personally, and I tried to dissuade him from sending more combat troops to Vietnam. At that time he reviewed for me the whole situation as he saw it, stressed how at a policy meeting with President Eisenhower he had opposed sending troops to Vietnam in 1954, how Eisenhower had sent aid and "advisors," how Kennedy had sent "more aid" and more "advisors," and how it was now his burden. He concluded by noting that the situation looked extremely black, and said: "I must either send troops or withdraw our advisors. And I am not going to be the first President to run." I did not think that was the issue, nor the right context for a decision of this importance, and I so told him.

And thus ends this dismal chapter in our history . . . or does it? I do not believe so. I think we are now about back where we started, only in deeper, and with hundreds of thousands of troops still in Vietnam and destined to remain there and hundreds of thousands more destined to be sent there. Though "Vietnamization" is for me preferable to the escalation of the previous administration, it has now been our policy since June, 1969, and one can only hope it succeeds—but it has surely failed to "end the war." Tragically we have suffered more than 60,000 casualties in the course of "Vietnamization" already.

And now that the conflagration threatens to engulf Laos and Cambodia, we may not be able to bring either peace or stability to South Vietnam until we are willing to *negotiate* a compromise settlement based upon genuine self-determination and a defined state of neutrality for the entire area in the ideological struggle between the major powers. As the first step, this requires that we cut the umbilical cord which binds us to the amoral junta in Saigon.

As I said at the beginning of this discussion, it is bitterly ironic and deeply tragic that in being willing to try to bring stability and peace to Indo-China after the defeat of the French there, we have been unable to evolve a workable solution which we ourselves can accept. We failed to understand many things about Vietnam, and one of them was that the divisions within the country were deep and old, long antedating our presence there. But however ignorant we were about this small country on the rim of Asia, I do believe we sincerely had a deep concern for the peace of the world. We hoped that settlement of the conflict there—as in other countries which were breaking free of their colonial status—would help create conditions conducive to peace throughout the world.

Peace throughout the world—and peace among ourselves—should be our highest purpose now, and remain our purpose.

Our frustration and sadness, our anguish and despair threaten our own national well-being. Our people deserve better.

2.

The Nation and the World

IT was Cordell Hull, a fellow Tennessean and townsman of mine, who towards the conclusion of his two massive volumes of memoirs remarked concerning the conduct of American foreign affairs:

> "Congress and the Executive have an inescapable responsibility to keep our foreign policy on a non-partisan basis. Partisan considerations have no place in foreign policy, for there the welfare and perhaps the future of the whole nation are at stake. It is always licit to criticize foreign policy, provided the critic honestly bases his argument on his conception of our national interests; but it is inadmissable to inject advantages of party or of person into foreign policy."

I embrace without reservation the above judgments, as I do much of the record of this great Tennessean who served longer as Secretary of State than any other man in our history. Nevertheless it must be pointed out that it has been in the very name of this "nonpartisan" basis that pressure has been exerted by the administration and its supporters which would, unless resisted, make of the United States Senate a merely *post-factum* corroborative body, a body, that is, whose only function in foreign affairs is to confirm the actions of the Executive.

Although the foreign affairs of our nation are *conducted* by the President, who also plays the leading role in formulating foreign policy, the Senate shares this latter office with the Executive. Under the constitutional mandate of "advise and consent," the Senate is equally responsible for those regulations which guide our relationship with other countries of the world: and this, by the ratification of treaties, by the confirmation of ambassadors and other personnel, by the appropriation of funds, by trade and tariff legislation, and by a number of other instrumentalities which I shall examine shortly.

Thus while the President is commander-in-chief of our armed forces, only the Congress is empowered to declare that state of war which would unleash those forces. Similarly, although the actual conduct of military engagements in a Congressionally authorized war devolves ultimately upon the Executive, the Congress exercises an indirect control, though a very effective one, over the military by passing judgment on all appropriations necessary to sustain it. That the Founding Fathers saw the need for the Congress to supervise closely the Executive in the conduct of war is emphatically illustrated by Thomas Jefferson's remark to James Madison in 1780: "We have already given in example one effectual check to the Dog of War by transferring the power of letting him loose from the Executive to the Legislative Body, from those who are to spend to those who are to pay."

To make our governmental system work at maximum efficiency, there must be a full exchange of information between the Executive and the Legislative; but this exchange should be—apart from classified matters—equally full and complete between the people and their elected representatives. My conviction that the Senate's one hundred members must take a new look at themselves and at the Senate as an institution, and manifest a new determination to exercise an expanding and changing responsibility in the everchanging and expanding role of the United States in world affairs was expressed publicly in 1969 at the ABM hearings, and also in the National Commitments Resolution which I strongly supported. In discussing this Resolution, I pointed out that the Senate's failure to act effectively in matters of foreign policy was not due in all instances to inherent defects in the structure of the Senate, but to a collective unawareness of its obligation as an independent, co-equal branch of government in the supervision of international affairs.

I went on to suggest that the Senate consider adding a new dimension to its function of advise and consent: a dimension not spelled out explicitly by the Founding Fathers, but for which the Constitution provides ample warrant. I envisioned a more active role for the Senate and for the American people in participatory democracy, a role which today's rapid means of communication and high educational levels now make much more possible than would have been the case in the early days of the Republic. I therefore proposed a massive involvement of the people in the decision-making processes by mobilizing an enlightened public opinion.

How often have I heard legislators exclaim in Washington: "If the people could only vote on this issue!" "If only there were better ways for them to involve themselves more effectively between elections!" It should be evident from my discussion of our Vietnam crisis that I don't like the notion of a "silent majority"—indeed, I think it a myth that neither exists nor deserves to be fabricated. We must seek out methods whereby citizens and their representatives may debate and discuss national issues before a national audience. The Congress is not only a legislative body, but an educative one as well, and I will continue to seek means whereby this latter function might be broadened. Our experience with the ABM and Vietnam issues has clearly proved that the Senate can be a strong influence for the clarification of public issues. At the televised hearings of the Senate Foreign Relations Committee in 1966 on the causes and conduct of the war in Vietnam, I stated: "We were unable to reach the President on this. Now we are going over his head—to the American people." And we did precisely that, and with great success. In fact, it was widely reported that as the televised hearings began President Johnson had two television sets in his office each tuned to a different network. Whether to divert public attention from the hearings—as widely reported at the time—or not, I cannot say; but at any rate the President quickly announced a trip to Hawaii to meet with South Vietnamese Premier Nguyen Cao Ky. Attention may have been partially diverted by such a maneuver, but nevertheless the hearings succeeded in having a profound impact on U.S. public opinion regarding the strategy, the legality, and the morality of our presence in Vietnam. I think those hearings may have saved us from another major escalation, and possibly even from war with China.

Similarly with the issue of deployment of an anti-ballistic missile system. Here was an Executive proposal which could have radically affected our entire foreign policy and also, in terms of domestic affairs, could have had grave consequences for the equitable allocation of our national resources. The debate over this proposal resulted in the first major conflict in the ongoing struggle to reorder our national priorities. As Chairman of the Foreign Relations Subcommittee on Arms Control, International Law, and Organization, I held exhaustive hearings behind closed doors with my colleagues on the Committee. They amassed a volume of information, enough in fact to cause a majority of them to oppose deployment of the ABM system which the military had convinced President Nixon was needed. I sought and won permission to hold public hearings, seminars really, on the issue. Aided by a competent staff, and enlisting the support of the intellectual community across the nation, we achieved an unprecedented involvement of our people in a decision bearing on an extremely sophisticated subject. Through these televised hearings, many millions of people, along with the members of the Senate itself, became students of this politico-strategic problem. What resulted was a truly informed national debate. The people reached their own judgments, and mail flooded the Congressional offices. It was a milestone in participatory democracy.

And why should this not become a more common practice? It is the people's lives, their country and their world which face the possibility of nuclear destruction; it is the people's resources which are to be allocated; it is the people's needs which are to be served. My feeling at the time was that whatever the outcome (a tie-vote broken in favor of the ABM system by Vice-President Agnew), this education of the nation under the guidance of elected representatives was in itself a magnificent achievement—and this regardless of the ultimate legislative result. We live in a troubled time when our people are uncertain of national goals in world affairs and are fearful of tomorrow. They deserve more access to more information on crucial problems.

Given this absolute imperative for greater public enlightenment, something more is required than merely public hearings in Washington where the nation can be informed only by concession of the television networks. Effective participatory democracy should not be dependent on the whim *or* on the considered judgment of the media executives who may *or* may not have a personal or corporate interest in this or that specific piece of legislation. Perhaps we ought to look at the experience of all other major industrialized countries where a national radio-television network—which in our case should be responsible to both the Legislative and Executive branches—airs all the major political problems. We need a "Voice of America" for Americans. Perhaps then the putative "silent majority" would find its proper voice. There are difficulties, of course, in the development of such a communications instrument, and safeguards would have to be made ironclad to obviate partisan control—but this would present no insoluble problem: we have similar such safeguards for any number of governmental agencies. And we may already have moved in this direction through educational television.

But assuming that this proposal is not immediately practicable, there must be found some effective educational method for the Congress to make participatory democracy a reality and not just a vague hope. One way might be to hold public hearings on the most important pending foreign-policy matters in selected major cities in various parts of the nation—in the past such hearings have generally been confined to purely domestic issues. This would guarantee network and press coverage accessible to millions of people in a given area since the media would never ignore a "local" event of such importance.

Without this evocation of national interest by the Congress, there is the ever-present danger that the control of political affairs will degenerate into government—in Woodrow Wilson's well-chosen words on an ill-chosen occasion—by "a little group of willful men." The Senate is partially at fault for not more vigorously exercising its leadership in vital educational functions. It is at fault, too, in relaxing its constitutional role in foreign affairs. We have consented when we should have advised. We have advised and consented on minor matters, countless postmaster confirmations, for instance, while neglecting the larger questions of foreign policy. We have bestirred ourselves only tardily—but I hope permanently—to reassert the constitutional responsibility of the Senate.

This is an unruly world of nearly 140 sovereign nations, many ripe for the outbreak of internal or regional warfare; we have treaties to defend 43 countries; we provide economic aid to over 70; military aid, to about 50; and our defense establishment prior to 1970 was predicated on an ability—in its careless jargon—to fight "two-and-one-half wars" at the same time. This has recently been reduced to "one-and-one-half wars." Clearly such an over-extension of our resources demands a re-ordering of priorities abroad as well as at home.

Although we may have interests around the world, they are obviously not of equal importance and we must learn to distinguish between what is essential to our well-being and what is only desirable. And having learned this we must learn also to graduate our response to challenges in accordance with their greater or lesser gravity. Vietnam, and now Laos and Cambodia, indicate that this is a lesson which has not been learned in some quarters of the government. "Massive retaliation" is a strategy that dies hard. There are still paleolithic strategists among us who want to blast every single enemy—whether he be great or small, significant or trivial—back into *their* own stone-age culture.

We cannot afford to maintain unlimited power in foreign affairs, and we cannot afford to entertain a primitive—and slightly demented—ambition for world domination. The truth is we have passed the time—if it ever existed—of a Pax Americana, in the sense that there was once a Pax Romana and a Pax Brittanica. No single nation today can either by its power or its prestige maintain the peace of the world. New trends and new forces have been unleashed upon us, and new facts of international life must be faced.

One of these facts is that the cold war as the dominant pattern in world politics has ended. In a simple dualistic political model—good *v.* bad, democratic-free world *v.* Communist imperialism—both elements are intrinsically antagonistic, and the one that dominates the other in effect dominates the world. Vietnam has invalidated this model, for the conflict there is certainly not between a purely democratic and a purely imperialistic power. It is a conflict clouded by areas of gray and by a multiplicity of factors which cancel out any crude black-white solution.

Thus the real "gap" about which we must be concerned is neither a missile gap nor a credibility gap: it is the gap between a world whose ideologies and national interests move across a whole spectrum of changing political hues, and our image of that world which is seen only in black-white terms—or rather in Red. It is the gap between what really exists and what our military planners imagine exists. While our attention was focused on Vietnam the world moved on, moved away from a period of polarization, toward an era of swift and constant change. In this polymorphous world, our foreign policy has been univocal—some would say monomaniac. Even President Nixon in his

"State of the World" declaration acknowledged these new forces at play on the international scene. Whether he can implement this knowledge through positive action remains to be seen. Knowledge without praxis is sterile.

This is a fluid world, a world of unprecedented ferment in which the movement of international politics must be flexible, less tied to the status quo, and less fixated on the issues of yesteryear. Our American position in regard to Communism now must be viewed in a broader world perspective because much of what has taken place in the world in the last decade has had little to do with Communism. This is certainly not to our disadvantage because it reflects a definite decline in the influence and power of Soviet imperialism. The primitive Soviet dream of a universal world revolution—stage-managed from the Kremlin—almost certainly has disappeared.

The U.S. of course still must have, and conceivably for a very long time, the capability to resist threats and pressures from antagonist power centers. A *sufficient* nuclear deterrent therefore still is needed. But we can no longer equate each failure in our foreign policy with a victory for Communism which requires, as compensation on our part, expansion of the nuclear arsenal. Rather we must recognize that the nuclear deterrent is in fact no deterrent whatever to the score of minor aggressive acts, rebuffs, and insults to which we may and likely will be subjected in the future.

We have been so busy focusing our sights on the predatory Soviet bear in the forest that we have not kept our eyes on the trees—nor indeed could we see that some of these were blossoming and bearing good fruit. The fact is that in the arenas of world opinion and of measurable achievement we have won considerable victories over Soviet imperialism in the last decade. Unfortunately this has not always resulted from our own direct action, although our actions—Vietnam clearly excepted—have for the most part been not unworthy of a great power. These "victories" have been the result of the fact that democracy, even when ill-managed, remains the strongest political ideology and the most effective moral force that the world has ever known. The American nation has traditionally been the embodiment of that ideology and that force.

Although we have seen this body politic, this embodiment of human aspiration, bruised and maimed in recent years, we must not lose faith in its fundamental health and soundness. Certainly it should be a matter of pride to all Americans that at the close of World War II this nation sought no territorial gains, sought to subject no other countries to its domination; it should be equally a matter of pride to us as free men that of the more than 60 new countries which came into being since the end of that war, none freely subjected itself to Soviet imperialism. All of them opted for democracy—usually for democratic socialism—as opposed to totalitarianism, because the concept of democracy with its emphasis on the dignity of the individual is the animating principle of all mankind. Democracy represents the "heart's desire" of humanity.

Not all these fledgling countries are democracies in our sense of the word with its connotation of a government of freedom within a framework of responsibility. But we above all, who have experienced the vicissitudes of demagoguery and the erosion of civil liberties, should know full well that while democracy is the best form of government, it is also the most difficult to manage. We understand the workings of democracy, and are most critical of its defects, because its spirit has been bred into us from our birth, and because we have had almost two centuries in which to refine its actual implementation—a task which is never ending. I mention all of this in the context of a discussion on international affairs because our only effective foreign policy must be founded on the most rigorous fidelity to the democratic ideal.

In a hall on the Senate side of the Capitol there is a bust of Cordell Hull—whom I will be referring to frequently in these pages. The legend on the bust reads, "Father of the United Nations"—a great epitaph for a great man who spent his life promoting this democratic ideal among the nations of the world through trade agreements, the good-neighbor policy, and finally—as Secretary of State—through the United Nations. Yet Hull would have been the last man in the world to sacrifice a vital national interest to any international body. He believed that the primary duty of any democratic nation was to guarantee its own life, to provide for its own security. With a typically American pragmatic idealism, Cordell Hull affirmed that it was in the self-interest of each nation to cooperate in promoting the welfare of the international community of nations.

The United Nations is an experiment in regulated internationalism, something towards which the countries of the world have haltingly been moving for generations. Already its life span exceeds that of the old League of Nations, which for all practical purposes ceased to function after two decades of turbulence and neglect. So long as the United Nations can demonstrate its usefulness, I am confident that it will continue. The existence of a world organization where debate and consultation among various countries can occur—indeed where debate can occur even between and among nations engaged in acts of open hostility—such a need is a demand of our time. One of the most indelible of my memories is of the meaningful and decisive U.N. debate between Adlai Stevenson and the Soviet Ambassador, Zorin, during the Cuban missile crisis. As a delegate to the U.N. at that time, I realized the importance of these two rival powers having a common forum in which to expose their differences.

Any organization fulfilling so delicate a role will invariably be the subject of strong criticism from its opponents and of exorbitant hopes from its supporters. Like any worldwide organization, the U.N. therefore must be on guard against both its bitter enemies and its over-zealous friends. The avowed enemies profess to see in the U.N. a force which will subordinate the United States to the rule of some alien power. But some of the over-zealous friends of the U.N., while rightly decrying such a misunderstanding of the organization by these fearful rightists, often display just as serious a misunderstanding by failing to realize that the U.N. endorses the concept of the nation-state, comes to grips with it, and operates within its framework.

Today we live, move, and function in an age of nationalism—and this is particularly true of the emerging countries in the "Third World." The nation-state is the most viable form of polity thus far devised; and any successful international body must accommodate itself to that fact, not only today but in the foreseeable future. I view with considerable trepidation any over-zealous advocacy of a world state.

In a justly renowned book of the early part of this century the historian Frederick Jackson Turner defined the role of the frontier in our history. As every student knows, he saw the frontier as fulfilling a creative function in our national development by allowing the discontented, dissident—the unassimilable "rugged individualists"—a place to exercise their abilities, and thus to act both as safety valve and as catalyst to the comfortable, established society behind the frontier. As a Tennessean, as a Senator from a state where these pioneer values of dissent and individualism are still treasured, I would fear the kind of closing of the "frontier" which any world government would entail, a government in which every citizen would be subject to world-wide surveillance and to a world-wide police authority. Fortunately the issue is mainly speculative: by the time we are likely to have a world state, it is just as likely that the moon will be our new "frontier." In the meanwhile we must live with the nation-state, and the United Nations is our most effective trans-national cooperative instrument.

The U.N. must operate on the principle of voluntary cooperation among independent, sovereign, and juridically equal peoples who in their own countries have organized themselves in widely different patterns for their own national purposes. Its "police function," for want of a better term, is limited to matters in which the majority powers concur. But even here its scope is strictly limited. Its most effective role, therefore, has been that of encouraging dialogue and ideological encounter. It is the anvil on which international conciliation can be hammered out.

It is a mark of great progress in civilization that we have taken even this step in cooperative measures. Unfortunately, too much emphasis has been placed on the U.N.'s peacekeeping efforts and not enough on its more positive achievements as a vehicle for human progress. Its agencies, including the International Refugee Organization, the Food and Agricultural Organization, the World Health Organization, and UNESCO, have worked closely with nations around the world—especially with developing nations—to improve health and sanitation, and to provide food and shelter for the needy.

Though the United Nations' positive humanitarian goals have been realized more fully than its negative ones, nonetheless it has made some direct contributions to world peace, for example by mediating the dispute over boundaries between India and Pakistan, by helping resolve our own Bay of Pigs fiasco, by enforcing truces in numerous African insurrections and tribal wars, by its action during the Korean War, and by assisting refugees throughout the world. True, it has not been very effective in the troubled Middle East, largely because of lack of sufficient cooperation between the United States and the Soviet Union. Yet, since both powers have major security interests there and deep political commitments, continued hostilities may generate a major confrontation.

Nevertheless, and here I digress briefly, the United States has a political affinity with Israel and a moral obligation growing out of its creation which cannot be dismissed. Failure of the U.N. to bring about cooperation between Israel and the Arab States, and lack of sufficient cooperation between the United States and the U.S.S.R.—along with the Soviet threat to accelerate the re-arming of Egypt—means that the United States must be ready to assist Israel in maintaining the strength necessary for her survival. Though U.N. efforts in the bitterly tragic situation of Israel have failed, such a failure does not really derogate from the over-all accomplishment of the organization. Despite its structural weaknesses and its obvious inadequacies there is no doubt that if we did not have the U.N., we would be forced to organize a similar such international body.

We have come a long way since the difficult days following the end of World War II when Stalin was in ruthless control of the Soviet Union and intent on expanding his empire both to the east and to the west, when China was about to fall—as it did—to Communism, and when the Berlin crisis was already in its incipient stages. Today, in contrast to all of that, the Soviet Union is governed by a new generation of bureaucrats, Communists to be sure, but

Communist technocrats who rule more pragmatically and more rationally, and who disclaim, at least publicly, any intention to conquer by force.

Today, Berlin is relatively secure. Greece, Turkey, and Iran—once threatened by the forces of Soviet hegemony—have maintained their independence. Today, the countries of Eastern Europe, though by no means free of Russian domination, are moving at different speeds away from a relationship of subservience and towards greater national control. The suppression of Czechoslovakia has made these other countries more cautious, but the events in Czechoslovakia displayed to the world how intoxicating is the appeal of democratic freedom even in a tightly controlled Soviet satellite. Today, the Congo, though a long way from being a viable democracy, is now at least approaching that condition of political stability where such democracy becomes practicable. Soviet power has not overrun South Korea and there is no apparent prospect that it will do so. Despite the alarmists and the domino theorists, Castro's ascendency in Cuba has not been followed by other Communist regimes in Latin America.

But it is precisely at this point that, in enumerating these considerable achievements of the past two and a half decades, I must point out our most disastrous failing: the identification of the United States—by its hasty embrace of one military dictator after another—with political repression abroad. The fruits of this ill-founded expedient are almost sure to be even more bitter in the future than they have proved to be in the recent past: witness Governor Rockefeller's hostile reception in Latin America in 1969. It is a tragic fact that political regimes in some countries to which our aid has been granted exist with but little or no discernible popular support and, in some at least, maintain themselves in power almost entirely by means of U.S.

assistance. This support we give to dictatorships is a matter of crass expediency which is rationalized by the naïve hope that the dictators whom we aid will become enlightened and will voluntarily bring about conditions under which democratic procedures can emerge. But the peoples who are oppressed by those whom we aid will not be swayed by —if indeed they can or should understand—such alleged subtleties of international power politics. All they know is that those who exercise arbitrary rule over them are supplied their guns by the United States.

I recognize that our government cannot deal directly with the individual citizens of a nation which is to receive our aid. If we are to deal at all, we must deal with the government which is in power—even the Red Cross, and the Protestant and Catholic relief agencies do this. Obviously, therefore, I do not in any way suggest that we must always choose to grant aid to a democratic government and never to an authoritarian regime. Would that international affairs were that simple! I am aware also that there is a limit beyond which we cannot go in attaching conditions to our aid, lest we subject ourselves to the charge that we are interfering in matters that quite properly must be determined by the recipient nation. Nor is it to be expected that we can create overnight democratic governments in countries where democracy is unknown and whose citizens are unprepared to discharge its responsibilities.

Nevertheless, while recognizing the arguments from expediency, the extension of aid to dictators under conditions which lead to the perpetuation of tyrannic regimes must be recognized as a contradiction of our long-range policy objectives. In the final analysis, the struggle we are engaged in is between the concept of freedom and the concept of despotism. A dictatorship of the right can be as oppressive as a dictatorship of the left. Moreover, in granting aid to authoritarian governments, we imperil even our short-range goals. If a despotic regime, which holds power either in whole or in part as a result of our aid, should be overthrown, the new revolutionary government will almost certainly not be well-disposed towards us. By virtue of our aid, we are identified in the minds of the people with the dictatorial rulers: if they go down, so do we.

The present state of our relations with Cuba is due in large measure to our previous alignment with the cruel and corrupt Batista regime. Whatever may have been our reasons for giving aid to Batista, we are in the minds of the Cuban masses identified with him and his government which, to say the least, did not deal justly with the Cuban people. Thus it is obviously no problem at all for Fidel Castro to ignite among the Cuban masses the flames of bitter anti-Americanism.

But the conduct of our foreign affairs has not only been imperiled by mistaken policy judgments on the part of our government, it has suffered as well from the voracious greed of private U.S. interests. This lust to profit from the tax-payer's foreign-aid dollar has helped undermine the whole AID program, and has promoted ill-conceived projects abroad and disenchantment at home. As this disenchantment with foreign aid has grown in the Congress, those with a vested interest in continuing assistance turned to so-called "banks" with soft-loan windows. That it was self-interest and not national interest, at least by some influences, which motivated this move makes it all the more necessary that we severely scrutinize such "loan" operations, operations which now constitute a large part of the AID program. Many of these "soft-loans"—which are in fact grants—were actually engineered by U.S. corporations with a view to abetting their own private goals.

This is one reason I opposed the "soft-loan" money for

the Inter-American Development Bank in 1967. The other reason is related to that matter of national priorities to which I have alluded throughout this chapter. The federal-loan programs for our *own* community improvements have been so curtailed that thousands of worthy project applications are unfunded. What could be the justification for 900 million dollars in never-to-be-repaid soft-loans to build facilities in Latin America when sound repayable loans for community improvements were being denied at home? I lost this fight in the Senate 65-21. Now, it is noteworthy that although this was during the Johnson Administration, twenty-nine Republican Senators voted or announced support for the 900-million-dollar loans, and only seven voted against.

As all of the previous discussion makes clear, I have been a vigorous critic of the excesses and errors in our foreign-aid program, both in the governmental and the private sectors; nevertheless in the over-all I have been a constant supporter of its underlying premise—both as a matter of political prudence and of morality. The industrialized nations of the world are obliged to assist the underdeveloped countries. My hope is that in the future such assistance will take the form of more people-to-people aid, and will be more concerned with social hygiene and education and with what might be called "self-help" projects. Thus despite the soft-loan excesses and the errors of judgment, the fruits of our programs have been generally beneficial.

It is to our great honor, I believe, that we recognized our moral and political bonds with the countries of Western Europe and other war-wracked, destitute countries such as Greece and Turkey, and that we helped other underprivileged countries to withstand the onslaught of Communism at a time when it was seeking to absorb them into the Soviet

Empire. Now that that world-wide threat of Soviet imperialism has diminished, we must base our assistance programs on a more positive and more disinterested moral mandate.

We have spent more than 60 billion dollars in aid programs to assist other countries—East and West—raise their living standards. This was a bold, generous action by a great people. The necessity of being both pragmatic and frugal now does not detract from the nobility of this achievement in the past nor diminish the necessity of further assistance in the future.

Equally as important as an effective aid program in strengthening the economic and social structure of other nations, and in forging the bonds of international cooperation, is our foreign-trade policy. A gigantic system of economic agencies, in all of which the U.S. has generally played a constructive role, has been established within this generation to foster such trade and development: the General Agreement on Tariffs and Trade, the World Bank, the International Development Association, the U.N.'s Development Program, and regional trade groupings among the nations of Europe, Latin America, and Asia.

By no means the least significant in these steps towards greater international cooperation has been our own Reciprocal Trade Program—fathered by Cordell Hull in the 1930's—which helped to resolve many of the difficulties brought about by the high protectionist tariff policies adopted under the Harding-Coolidge-Hoover administrations after World War I. This program has enjoyed a remarkable success, and under it the United States has pioneered in showing other nations the benefits which can accrue to the world community from an expanded international trade.

I don't want to see that enlightened program destroyed by this or by succeeding administrations. And let us not be deceived, higher tariffs and protectionism are—and I mean this literally—Republican *trademarks*. Especially will the cry for more protection arise now that our foreign-trade balance is diminishing. In the early 1960's this country was selling abroad, on an annual average, between 5 and 6 billion dollars more in products than we were importing. In 1968 that differential fell to less than one billion dollars. At a superficial glance this would seem to be a potentially catastrophic situation and the protectionists—true to their nature—would like to capitalize on it. But in fact this does not mean that we have lowered our export rate, which continues to increase by 8 to 10 per cent a year; rather, it is that exports are not increasing as rapidly as imports which last year went up 24 per cent. There is nothing irremediable about such a rise: it merely indicates that other nations are following our own lead in expanding their foreign trade. Unfortunately some American industries—agriculture, textiles, the manufacture of bicycles and shoes, for instance—have suffered serious setbacks as a result of this competition from abroad. This must be solved—as I am convinced it can be—without excessively restrictive import prohibitions, and with regulations controlling the outflow of American capital and with voluntary bilateral agreements. Without this, import restrictions are necessary.

Most bills introduced in Congress as a "remedy" would set up a system of quotas for imports. But such a solution to the dilemma will have an even more adverse effect on the national economy than did the old-fashioned high tariff system. If we cut imports, we will immediately be placed on a retaliatory see-saw with other countries which, in turn, will stop exports. We must bear in mind that the United States world export trade is still nearly 20 per cent of the whole—and this means many more thousands of jobs for Americans than could ever be salvaged by adopting a series of *ad hoc* quota systems which would have to undergo constant and endless revision to keep them in line with the fluctuations of the market. The regulation of such a system would prove almost impossible. The bi-partisan Randall Commission which studied our trade policies and wrote an exhaustive report on them noted that 4 million American jobs are directly involved in the manufacture and production of our exports, and—more significantly—the Commission pointed out that this number could be increased only if we avoid excessively restrictive practices.

I recall when Premier Khrushchev bragged that "We will bury you"—and then explained that he really meant he would defeat us in the "peaceful war of trade." Americans may not have taken that boast seriously, but the Russians have become a major trading nation, and, of course, since their government controls production and pricing, they can frequently offer more favorable terms than their competitors. We cannot evade the harsh economic reality that we must both increase our exports and arrive at agreements with countries which are now introducing too many goods into our domestic market. As an example, I would point to the voluntary agreement, which I was instrumental in negotiating, whereby Japan limited her cotton textile exports to the United States, extension of which she now resists.

Obviously, then, I am not opposed to all tariffs since, as the Randall Commission estimated, if all tariffs were removed it would mean an increase in unemployment in this country of close to 200,000 workers. I favor increased exports and adjustments which I believe can be worked out with other nations regarding particular excessive imports into this country. The difference between what I am advocating and what the advocates of protectionist quotas are advocating is that, in the first instance, it is this country which unilaterally raises barriers against certain imports;

whereas, in the second instance, it is the government of the exporting foreign country which imposes its *own* type of restriction on its *own* manufacturers and producers. Moreover, in the trade laws we presently have, there are provisions made to assist American companies and employees that lose work because of competing imports. These provisions have not been extensively used to date, and unfortunately they are not, as they ought to be, fully compensatory.

But after all the statements of economic philosophy, and all the techniques of economic practice have been explored, we end up with the simple truism that a nation cannot sell unless it buys. This is a principle not only in the economic, but also in the political order. Friendship follows the trade routes. And here once again I would quote Cordell Hull:

> "High tariffs do not bring us prosperity. They do bring us unsalable surpluses at home and the resentment of other nations abroad.
>
> "The people of the states in which special interests demand high tariffs of an embargo nature should understand this. They should know that one successful attempt to put a stone on the high-tariff wall in favor of one product inevitably leads to similar attempts to put many more stones on the wall in favor of other products. Let them, as consumers, keep their Congressmen advised that the interests of the people at large are superior to those of the comparatively few industrial and agricultural interests that clamor for 'protection.'
>
> "And let the Members of Congress appreciate the still higher issue involved—our cooperation with other nations. We cannot erect high-tariff walls around our nation and expect to cooperate, politically or economically, with the rest of the world."

Our exports can mean the difference between prosperity and recession, between a high level of employment for

American workers and widespread national unemployment. Our farmers particularly are faced by a permanent crisis unless we can find some way to increase the market for our agricultural commodities, commodities which the thousands of starving people in the nations of the underdeveloped Third World are crying out for.

The United States cannot stand alone economically any more than it can politically and militarily. The American free-enterprise business man is alleged to be the most efficient commercial operator in the world; and I suppose he is. He is alleged to thrive and grow prosperous on competition; and I believe competition is healthy. But some of these businessmen grow livid with rage at the prospect of competition from small foreign suppliers. So true is this that they have made foreign investments to compete with their own U.S. products: a uniquely perverse notion of "competition" and "free enterprise"! For such businessmen, competition is laudable on the domestic front, but not on a multinational basis—unless, of course, they are allowed to play the game from both sides. But the majority of them are not willing, or perhaps are merely not able, to invest and manufacture abroad; and they are therefore exerting all their efforts to elect high protectionists to House and Senate. If they do succeed in this tactic, it will mean the end of the tenuous but nonetheless effective mutual trade relations we have developed over the past decades. Even more it will mean the atrophy of one of the most effective arms of our foreign policy, which can only be postulated on an ever greater and greater cooperation among nations.

I turn now to the most snarled and knotty problem facing this democratic society as it pursues this goal of international cooperation: our future relations with the two great Communist powers, Russia and China.

One of the most significant trends of the past two decades has been the realization among the citizenry and in government circles of both the United States and the Soviet Union that these two great powers have many interests in common. Not only are they the two leading military powers, the two leading industrial powers, with the two highest gross national products, they are also the two leading nuclear powers. This latter fact, ironically enough, gives them a vital stake in preserving the peace, for any nuclear war would be bound to destroy both nations. We have come too close to war—in Berlin, in Korea, in Cuba, in the Middle East, and in Vietnam—for any sane man to want to perpetuate the conditions of bitter hostility.

But, of course, I do not want to imply that all the fundamental and dangerous problems existing between the two countries have been swept away. There is a basic ideological antagonism between them that undoubtedly will exist for years to come and will inhibit amicable relations. The burden of past grievances, broken promises, and hostile action, is a heavy one. But the course of recent history itself reflects this common desire for harmony: the partial test-ban treaty, the non-proliferation agreement, the consular convention treaty, and the exchange programs in commercial and cultural fields—the latter particularly significant because they allow people-to-people encounters, and thus exorcise the devils of mistrust and hatred which the propaganda of both countries has too long fomented.

There are three great "spheres of influence" in the world of today: America, Russia, and China. Whether we like it or not, history will dictate that this tri-partite condition will be even more evident in the world of tomorrow. In that world, we shall realize fully what we now discern only vaguely, that our security and the world's safety depend in the final and most important analysis, first, upon relations between the United States and the two other great nuclear powers; and second, upon the force of world public opinion ever better informed through greater and greater mass communication systems. As President Eisenhower shrewdly observed, the people of the world are not going to let their governments stand in the way of world peace.

Neither peace nor our own security will then depend upon efforts on our part to establish at any and all costs governments made in our own image throughout the world—however pleasing to us in the short-range view that accomplishment might be. Equally, the giant Communist countries shall learn that neither their own prestige nor their own internal peace, neither the solidarity nor the security of the Communist bloc, will be achieved by aggression or military force. Though military power will be concentrated among three nations whose ideological characteristics may vary and change, the use of force by one of these nations to work its political will upon smaller countries will prove counter-productive if not totally abortive.

The United States, to its great honor, has generally realized this elementary fact and has generally acted accordingly. Thus, while we intervened in Korea where the issue of peace or war was clearly drawn by a massive armed attack from the North, we did not intervene in East Berlin in 1953, in Hungary in 1956, in Tibet in 1966, in Rhodesia in 1967, or in Czechoslovakia in 1968. Though the limited intervention in the Dominican Republic by the United States succeeded in preserving something of the status quo there, its cost in prestige and in improved hemispheric relations was severe—and both its need and justification are in serious doubt. We have not intervened in Haiti, or in Angola, or in Greece, or in Argentina, or in Nigeria, or in many other countries for the sake of preserving democracy and freedom. Where we have intervened we have done so not with a view to *establishing* democratic rule but rather with a view to *preventing* Communist domination, or to thwart a real or imagined Communist threat. We must, therefore, turn our wills and our energies to the principal objective of our foreign policy which is to maintain international peace among the three powers, and we must not be distracted from that overriding objective by primitive ambitions to rule everybody everywhere.

The war in Vietnam has not healed the breach between the Soviet Union and Communist China. As I have said in the previous chapter, we can take no credit for this continued contention between them. On the contrary, by all logic the war should have driven these two Communist powers into alliance, even against their traditional antipathies. But the breach between them has been too wide, and its roots too deep to be so easily repaired. The Chinese have had centuries of hostile relations with Russia. They have lost large parts of their territory to Russian domination. And the Chinese, both because of their strong national pride and their bitter resentment of the West, were bound to find such Russian domination hateful. Thus it is not surprising that Soviet "revisionism" may now rival, perhaps may now even have replaced, American "imperialism" as the principal object of Chinese hostility.

But while the Vietnam war has not restored unity between Russia and China, it has nevertheless joined them in a rivalry—a rivalry that is undesirable from our point of view but inevitable from theirs: they have become rivals to see which nation can appear to be the most anti-American and thus the most loyal defender and persuasive advocate of pristine Communist ideals. In this weird contest of orthodoxies, China now seems to hold some sort of lead.

If we terminate our involvement in Vietnam, it should

be possible for the United States to extricate itself from its position as the hostile target of Soviet-Chinese competition. We should be able, instead, to become the object of Soviet-Chinese competition for harmony with us. Good relations with the United States should become a precious asset to be sought rather than a pernicious attachment to be shunned. In short, the differences between the Soviet Union and China should work to our advantage and to that of world peace, instead of disadvantage.

We should therefore not encourage Soviet-Chinese hostility, whatever *immediate* benefits that course of action might appear to promise. Given the opportunity to play one nation off against the other—hardly an unforeseeable temptation—we would in the long run, it seems to me, be imperiling our own security. For if hostility between the Soviets and the Chinese were sufficiently aggravated, it would lead ultimately to a war between two of the greatest nations in the world, a war which would involve one third of the earth's population, a racial war, and one, lastly, which would involve two nuclear powers. But not taking the side of the Soviets in their feud with the Chinese does not mean that we could not find a common interest with the Soviets in restraining the Chinese. And, conversely, not supporting the Chinese in their argument with the Soviets does not mean that we could not encourage and help the Chinese to become even more independent, particularly economically independent.

Our relations with the Soviet Union were gradually improving before the United States adventure in Vietnam, and before the Soviet aggression in Czechoslovakia. These have been severe setbacks that threaten the achievements and cooperation that have been realized in nuclear test suspension, nuclear non-proliferation in outer space, and in cultural exchanges. Nevertheless the mutuality of interest that has developed cannot be overlooked. It should be possible, then, to pick up the threads of *détente* and undertake with caution and care to weave a more solid relationship with the Soviet Union. We should be able to increase contacts of many sorts—cultural, technological, informational, and academic. We should be able to develop an increasingly unfettered trade; and we should be able to make more progress towards agreements on further arms-control measures —as I will outline in the next chapter. Lastly, and more disinterestedly, we should be able to work towards joint efforts for the good of other nations: in economic assistance to the developing countries, in population control, and in space exploration.

But our relations with Communist China after Vietnam will be infinitely more complicated. Perhaps the first obstacle to be overcome is the widely held view in the United States that China is an expansionist power which is determined to tyrannize all of Asia. Now, it does not seem to me that the present Chinese government has shown much eagerness to spread its political faith by force. Communist China has, of course, promised to encourage and support wars of national liberation, but it has *not* promised to participate in those wars—and in fact, it has not done so. There is no doubt that the Peking government hopes that such wars will succeed not only in Vietnam, but in Laos, Thailand, Burma, and in other Asian countries as well. But we must not put more emphasis on their words than on their actions. We have confused their desire to see such wars succeed—a desire which is certainly no stronger than our desire to see such wars fail—with their ability or will to *insure* success.

But even if China does not threaten today, will she threaten tomorrow when she will have developed her nuclear capabilities and when she will have a sophisticated intercontinental ballistic missile force? I doubt whether we should quake at this prospect, given our awesome nuclear superiority. Possession of nuclear weapons is likely to prove to be as sobering to China as it has proved to be to the Soviet Union. If so, China may then be more nearly willing to approach her foreign problems in a reasonable and realistic fashion. We should not forget that Soviet-American relations were poorest when the United States had a monopoly of nuclear weaponry, and that they improved only in the period since a nuclear power balance has existed. In fact, the balance has created a kind of *détente* in Europe. There is no reason for not assuming that it could have a similar effect in Asia.

As far as Peking is concerned, the Nationalist Government of Taiwan is by far the most serious obstacle standing in the way of normalizing relationships with the United States. The principal source of the mainland government's resentment is that since 1950 we have been the chief supporter and advocate of the claims of the Nationalists. Surely we should, in the interests of peace in Asia, turn the various problems that revolve around Taiwan over to the Chinese themselves, the Chinese on the mainland and the Chinese on Taiwan. We should continue to insist that these problems be resolved peacefully, and we should leave no doubt that we will continue to honor our 1954 treaty to defend Taiwan against *armed* attack.

But it should not be beyond the ingenuity of the Chinese to arrange solutions to their various problems which would satisfy the demands of the 2 million mainland Chinese on Taiwan. The latter surely do not wish to continue to base their existence on the tragi-comic fiction that they alone are the true and certified Chinese people. Nor can the interests of the 11 million Taiwanese, who naturally do not wish to be governed permanently by 2 million non-

Taiwanese refugees, be ignored in reaching a solution to this problem. And in like manner, the mainland Chinese, notwithstanding their apparent disinclination at present to enter into more normal relationships with other countries, do not wish to see the unresolved problem of Taiwan perpetually obstruct their assumption of a more appropriate and positive role in Asia. Lastly, the other Asian nations, whose security is surely not enhanced but threatened by the bitter antipathies aroused by this issue, assuredly do not wish to see a continuation of this potentially explosive situation.

Thus all of these factors converge on the one point of the absolute necessity of our radically readjusting our relationship with Communist China. The commendable, though timid, steps towards reconciliation with China taken by President Nixon are but a start on this new course. As a next step, the United States should acknowledge—as clearly, unqualifiedly, and openly as possible, and at the highest level—that the government of the People's Republic *is* the government of China. And we should add that we are ready to exchange diplomatic representation with China and to negotiate mutually advantageous trade agreements. At the same time, we should desist from exerting a self-defeating pressure among our allies in the United Nations regarding the admission of China to that body. Communist China has, of course, fixed certain conditions to be met before she will be willing to join the U.N., including the expulsion of the United States. But these conditions are almost certainly a matter of propaganda only, and they are in fact so extreme that they would never be met by the United Nations. Nevertheless, why should the onus of Chinese intractability be borne by the United States? If the Chinese wish to protract their unreasonable, bellicose demands, then let them bear the burden of their own intransigence. We should urge China to qualify for membership in the family of nations and we should assist her in achieving this qualification.

There are two minor problems involving mainland China—far simpler problems than those of recognition and representation in the United Nations—which it should be possible for the United States to resolve immediately. One is travel, and the other is trade.

The total absence of travel between the two countries has created a barrier of ignorance and has spawned needless mutual hostility. Such a barrier serves the interests of neither nation. The Chinese themselves were the first to suggest in 1956 that American journalists visit China—an offer that we rejected. When we decided a year later to accept, they, understandably, had changed their minds; and they have since shown no disposition to remove the obstacles to free travel. Nevertheless, I see no reason to continue to insist on any reciprocal Chinese action—that is, on any procedure involving an offer by us and an acceptance by them on this point. If the Chinese remain unwilling to admit American journalists, doctors, scientists, and tourists, it will be their loss far more than it is ours. On the other hand, I believe that we should announce that we will validate passports for legitimate cultural, economic, and professional travel by Chinese in the United States. By this unilateral action we would have much to gain and nothing to lose.

As far as trade is concerned, it seems to me that the present situation verges on the ridiculous. It is doubtful whether our original objective of an embargo on all foreign trade with China by all non-Communist nations would really have caused sufficiently serious economic damage to China to force it to make concessions of some sort. Certainly such an embargo could not have caused the Communist regime to collapse. But, in any case, the question of the effect of such an embargo is academic, because other nations were not willing to join in imposing it. Peking's chief trading partners are the United Kingdom, Japan, the Soviet Union, West Germany, Australia, Canada, Italy, and France—all, with one exception, *our* allies.

While our refusal to allow American companies, or foreign subsidiaries of American companies, to trade with mainland China—even in non-strategic goods—has had little economic effect, it has had serious political repercussions. It has been a constant source of friction with our allies who regard our policy as misconceived, if not demented. And it has contributed another poisonous element to the atmosphere between the Chinese and ourselves.

I see no reason to trade in non-strategic items with the Soviet Union and the European Communist countries but not to trade *at all* with China. On the contrary, I see only benefits flowing from our increasing China's non-strategic trade with us and with other non-Communist countries. Trade is, after all, China's only window to the world today; it is her basic medium of international communication. United States trade has had positive political results in the Soviet Union and in Eastern Europe, and I see no reason to assume that similar results would not follow in China. As I have noted earlier, friendship follows the trade routes.

Unfortunately, there is a very real possibility that even after Vietnam such actions as I have advocated will not be welcomed—much less reciprocated—by the Chinese. The Chinese now look at the world through Marxist glasses with Maoist lenses, lenses which magnify traditional Chinese suspicions and resentments of other nations, and in a particular way, distort the Chinese view of the United States. These lenses could, of course, be removed, but it seems that China's present leaders feel they serve a useful purpose in generating fear among their own people and so making them less prone to question their government's policies.

Nevertheless logic and an enlightened long-range view of *our* own self-interest indicate that the United States should take the actions I have suggested rather than continue to attempt to compete on *their* terms with a group of political leaders who seem at present to be making a habit of ugly intransigence and a virtue of contentiousness.

Some may argue that it would be wiser to begin with very small steps, with exploratory negotiations, for example, or with some ingenious and intricately designed probe to discover whether the Chinese are prepared to respond to our initiatives. But such an undertaking might take years, and in the end serve only to exacerbate the situation. As a great power, founded upon the great moral principles of democratic freedom, we should be able to take ethically validated and politically prudent chances.

The truth is that the issue of our future relations with China and the Soviet Union is of such paramount importance that excessive caution is tantamount to excessive risk. For those in the United States who are still obsessed with the "menace" of Communism, who fear that it will sweep across the Atlantic and the Pacific to the shores of this country, such small steps will be just as incomprehensible —and thus just as unacceptable—as giant strides.

We are much more ready to quote George Washington's warning against "permanent alliances with any portion of the foreign world" and we are to cite his equally pertinent warning about "permanent, inveterate antipathies against particular nations." The prescient father of this country went on to say: "The nation which indulges towards another an habitual hatred, or an habitual fondness, is in some degree a slave. It is a slave to its animosity or to its affection, either of which is sufficient to lead it astray from its duty and its interest." The United States has been lead astray by its obsession with Communism. It has been led astray by an antipathy that has proved inveterate and a hatred that has become habitual—we *are* in danger of becoming the slaves of our animosities. Now is the time to purge ourselves. For if our relations with the Soviet Union and China and their relations with us do not begin to improve, but continue to deteriorate, the next war may be the world's last war.

As I began this chapter with a quotation from Cordell Hull, so I will end it:

> "Major wars are generally followed by a widespread feeling of uneasiness, impatience, unrest, and suspicion. Our people and leaders and the peoples and leaders of other nations must be willing to overcome this feeling. They must examine with sympathy and patience the views of others. They must try to ascertain the true facts in any situation. They must avoid assuming adamant positions. They must refrain from exaggerating and overemphasizing their own claims and from appealing to prejudice."

3.

Arms and the People

SINCE those two fateful days, August 6 and 9, 1945, when American planes dropped atomic bombs on Hiroshima and Nagasaki, the United States and the Soviet Union have engaged in what is potentially the most suicidal military struggle ever known to man. Like two mad, and often seemingly half-blind giants, they have piled nuclear armaments on top of nuclear armaments, and together have spent nearly a trillion dollars each in trying to get the better of the other.

The weapons that have been engendered by this mad race to see which nation can lure the other into the abyss are now many hundreds of times more destructive than those which in 1945 caused more devastation in a shorter length of time than the world had ever previously experienced. As if in a saga left over from the Dark Ages, the two powers seemed to have delighted in counting up their kilotons and megatons each night after the world had gone to bed and chalking up a victory sign at the birth of each new and more destructive weapon. The entire course of events for the innocent bystanders, that is, the people of the globe, assumed the dimensions of some vast cosmic nightmare in which humanity found itself again and again being hurled down into a chasm of hopeless destruction. Against the background of the awesome mushroom cloud, the cold war terrified people everywhere.

Always, good news for one rival power was bad news for the other; that *we* had the "bomb" made *them* want their own; *their* Sputnik frightened *us; their* alleged superiority in missiles made us not only seek to close the "gap" but to open it again—only in *our* favor; *their* ABM meant our MIRV and *our* ABM. The very terms "we" and "they," "ours" and "theirs," "us" and "them" seemed to provide sufficient justification for insoluble hatreds—insoluble except by *our* destruction of *them,* or vice versa: mistrust was the only apparent common ground between the two powers. It was a rivalry in folly.

But time passed, passions subsided, and hatreds were dissipated, as the two rival giants emerged from nuclear adolescence into something approximating maturity and parity.

It is perhaps, therefore, understandable why the two countries were unable to meet and take any mutually beneficial action until the early 1960s. But notwithstanding some small steps towards peace during that decade, there is still no firm assurance that the prospect of a nuclear holocaust is less likely now than it was a decade ago. Our present feeling that affairs are much more stable may be merely due to our having grown more accustomed, more hardened, to living on the cliff's edge. Indeed, an entire generation has been born and reared in the shadow of that first mushroom cloud.

Nevertheless, there has been some progress achieved in retreating from universal Armageddon. Both the partial test-ban treaty and the Nuclear Non-Proliforation Treaty are now in force. Also, the first bilateral treaty, the Consular Convention, and the Outer Space Treaty have been signed and approved by the Senate. Many cultural exchanges as well as some trade relations have been established. There is, thus, some small hope that other more positive steps will follow.

The "rite of passage" that may have launched us into adulthood was the Nuclear Test Ban Treaty signed on August 5, 1963, and ratified for the United States on October 10 of that year. As of the beginning of 1970, more than 100 countries were parties to this treaty. This is, by definition, a limited agreement, and its limitations have been well understood by both sides; but it is nevertheless an important step towards full maturity. It has radically reduced the number of tests in which otherwise both powers would certainly have engaged. *Our* bombs and *theirs,* would surely now be more destructive were it not for the mutually accepted sanctions that the treaty enforced.

More concretely, by stopping atmospheric tests, dangers to the health of both nations, including that of unborn generations, have been radically averted. In the fifties and early sixties the most potentially dangerous augmentation of pollution over the surface of the earth was coming not from industrial wastes or other manufacturing processes, but from contamination of the atmosphere by radioactive fallout. True, it will be decades before the effects of bombardment from strontium-90, the deadly bone destroyer, will no longer be harmful. But Iodine-131 has already virtually disappeared from our milk supply.

The treaty, limited and incomplete as it is, has had a healthy impact on recruitment of other members into the nuclear groups, on the expansion—to use the terminology of our casual strategists—of "the nuclear club." And the treaty did prepare the way for further negotiations. Psychologically, it has proved to be what President Kennedy hoped it would be, an important opening wedge in our effort to "get the genie back into the bottle."

As noted in the preceding chapter, no one can doubt that our relationships with the Soviet Union are more amicable today than a decade or more ago—though on the other hand neither is there any doubt that suspicion and distrust between the two nations still exist, and that the differences between their philosophies of government and of society will form a basis for continued conflict. These differences make agreements between the two countries almost unbelievably complex—more than 5000 negotiating sessions since the end of World War II—and each party, understandably, seeks to write into any agreement virtual guarantees for its own safety. Some of these guarantees, which are certainly understandable given the intense mistrust and hatred of the past, make it possible to conduct comprehensive, and continuing underground tests; to maintain nuclear laboratory facilities; to maintain the resources and facilities necessary for prompt resumption of atmospheric tests; and to improve the capability of detecting treaty violations. Caution for our own security dictates these reservations for us, and vice versa for them.

On our part we could hardly have sensibly considered not requiring these safeguards in view of the delicate balance of terror that prevailed during the sixties. Few will soon forget—I never will—the tremor of shock throughout the world when on October 23 and 30, 1961, the Soviets exploded nuclear devices in the 25 and 50 megaton range —the largest man-made destructive power ever unleashed. And all of this occurred when we believed there was a mutual understanding on a moratorium on testing. As a member of the Joint Committee on Atomic Energy, I am quite aware of this side of the picture, and of the necessity for caution. But as chairman of the Arms Control Subcommittee of the Foreign Relations Committee, I remain acutely conscious of the dismal and unsettling fact that the nuclear arms race continues and that negotiations with the Soviets remain problematic. If one must resolve this dilemma, as one must, it can only be through the realization that excessive caution ought never to jeopardize reasonable negotiations.

And I am profoundly convinced that any such future negotiations are in grave danger of being undermined by insistent proposals for the deployment of an anti-ballistic missile weapons system. I have, therefore, publicly deplored and criticized the decision of the Nixon Administration to snatch up this discredited and partially discarded Johnson program. To me such an action was tantamount to turning back the clock, and meant a step away from arms control and perhaps therefore from peace.

President Johnson had recommended an ABM system—called the "Sentinel"—as a possible defense against a Chinese missile attack. The idea was not well received in the area of three of our larger cities, around Boston, Chicago, and Seattle. City-dwellers and suburbanites alike, who were not much impressed by the imminence of the Chinese threat, did not want nuclear weapon installations of questionable effectiveness, and possible accidental dangers, cluttering up their landscapes. President Johnson's successor hoped to sell his product under the brand name "Safeguard," a more appealing label, it was thought, than "Sentinel." If space allowed, one might profitably disgress here on the need for a "truth-in-packaging" law since, thus far, Mr. Nixon has not made clear whether his more or less "invisible shield" of ABMs will in fact *safeguard* us against Russia, against China, or against the accidental firing of a missile by someone unknown. He has thus far not even settled on whether his system is to be an area defense, "thin" or "thick" —as the strategists say—or merely a "spot" safeguard for a few of our offensive missiles.

I have referred to President Nixon and "his" system, but perhaps I should more accurately refer to it as the Pentagon's project. But, of course, as always, it is the people's system—in fact their millstone. The cost has been estimated at upwards of $8 billion for the original "teaser" system, while a defense system even partially effective against any conceivable attack would cost truly astronomical amounts.

It was against this background of confusion and contradiction, of costly error and of gross danger, that I recommended that the Arms Control Subcommittee take the issue to the people in public hearings—as I have detailed in the preceding chapter. The result of that national debate was an unprecedented public involvement in a technical issue. President Nixon won his go-ahead when the tie vote was broken by the Vice-President, Mr. Agnew. After so vigorous a battle and so close a vote, one would have thought the Administration would hardly dare only a few months later to ask for a considerably expanded ABM system, yet it did. The Administration itself thus seemed to be validating the charge that its earlier request for only two sites was in fact a planned foot-in-the-door maneuver.

In his original request for "Safeguard" in a press conference on March 14, 1969, the President advanced three principal reasons in defense of its necessity: first, protection of our land-based Minuteman and SAC bases; second, protection against accidental launch from another country; and third, a "thin" area defense against possible Chinese attack. All the Defense Department witnesses stressed before the Subcommittee the role of "Safeguard" in protecting Minuteman siloes. The Administration also emphasized its plans for a "Phased Deployment Program," and affirmed that expansion of the system would be proposed only after there had been a thorough review of the knowledge gained from the experiences at the two initial locations. It was made clear by Administration spokesmen that only through such experience could an understanding of the integration of individual components into an operational system be gained. On the other hand, Administration critics pointed out that once a decision were made, flexibility to introduce changes would be greatly impeded and, moreover, a system installed at the missile sites cannot be tested against real missiles. Therefore, we suggested that actual intercepts be tested at Kwajalein.

There were a year ago, and there still are, other sharply critical technical questions which have never been answered satisfactorily by the Defense Department. For example, the "Safeguard" ABM system depends upon a single, very expensive (200 million dollars) radar for each Minuteman complex, with a small number—the number is still classified —of Sprint missiles to protect the Siloes, and an even smaller number to protect the radar.

But failure of the radar or its destruction would mean collapse of the whole operation. This problem was compounded by the fact that the Soviet Union's more cheaply developed and numerous SS-11 missiles, while *not* of sufficient explosive power and accuracy to endanger our siloes, are of sufficient power to destroy the radar installations. The missile-site radar, then, was much "softer" and thus easier to destroy than the siloes it was supposed to protect. This was the weak point of the whole concept of the ABM, a weakness obviated by the more traditional strategy of "diversity in deterrents" whereby the missiles would be widely dispersed and therefore a sufficient number would remain operational and could retaliate for any conceivable enemy attack.

The final argument, which the Administration has also thus far failed to counter, is based on the fact that the "Safeguard" system, in order to be reliable, must be in a constant state of readiness, and therefore dependent on the most highly sophisticated computer systems. Such refinement of computer technology, which was gravely doubted a year ago, is even more dubious now. And since we have had no experience with actual deployment upon which to base any further expansion, I cannot see that the Administration has proved or even strengthened its case.

Moreover, evidence indicates that if the threat of the Soviet SS-9—a much more powerful weapon than the SS-11—against the Minuteman siloes greatly increases, then the ability of "Safeguard," "thick" or "thin," to protect the missiles from nuclear assault would be entirely cancelled out. Thus dispersion and/or mobility remains the only effective deterrent strategy. And if it could be proved that the Soviets were targeting SS-9 missiles against all of our Minuteman siloes, some other tactic, perhaps mobile Minuteman or more submarine missiles, would necessarily have to be considered.

It is true that some technical witnesses had testified that an effective defense of the siloes against SS-9 attack could be made by employing many small radar systems rather than one large one; which, of course, would obviously render the entire defensive operation less susceptible to failure. Nor would a system of this kind have to play the dual role of hard-point defense (that is, defense of our offensive deterrent weapons) and population defense at the same time, and therefore would not be a threat to the Soviet deterrent—a perfectly legitimate argument that President Nixon stressed when choosing the "Safeguard" system over Johnson's "Sentinel."

Nevertheless, should the Soviet deployment of SS-9 missiles create an imbalance in the deterrent ratio—which cannot now be ruled out unless controls are agreed upon at the Strategic Arms Limitation Talks (SALT) Conference —then, as I have said, something other than ABM deployment would appear far more effective, far less risky, and perhaps even necessary. I suggest that mobile offensive power would have a greater deterrent effect upon both Russia and China than an untested anti-ballistic missile defensive system. And it goes without saying that the American people are surely more concerned about Soviet intercontinental ballistic missiles and nuclear submarines than they are about her own anti-ballistic missile sites around Moscow. And presumably the same is true of the Russian people and their leaders.

I had the impression throughout the hearings that Secretary Melvin Laird's arguments indicated he believed the way to stop an arms race is to *win* it. Indeed, I suspected that the real motivation may have been to gain a bargaining position against the Soviets, which is precisely the reason Johnson, according to Vice-President Humphrey, advocated the "Sentinel" ABM system.

I pointed out to the Secretary that with the multiple warheads being developed for our missiles, the United States would soon have 6500 thermonuclear weapons constantly on the alert and on the move in our submarine fleet, in addition to 3000 landbased missiles. In addition we have 1000 nuclear warheads ready to be delivered by bombers, as well as 7000 "tactical" nuclear weapons in Europe. No conceivable number of Soviet anti-ballistic missile systems could constitute a real shield against all these nuclear weapons. The ultimate absurdity of the Administration proposal is obvious to anyone who has not entirely abandoned simple mathematics and logic: no attack from any foreign country or combination of countries could in the foreseeable future neutralize a nuclear force of this strength and diversity.

The most disturbing aspect of this almost irrational advocacy of ABM is its possible effect on the larger issues of our foreign policy, and this not merely in terms of the dangers of any nuclear escalation, but even more so with regard to the premises on which our entire strategic posture is based. It is my belief that President Nixon raised very serious questions about our basic postulate of retaliatory deterrence by his statement on January 31, 1970, that the "Safeguard" system should be expanded in order to provide a "credible foreign policy in the Pacific area." He went on to add that such an area defense would be "virtually infallible"—the latter phrase one can charitably interpret as merely an instance of *ad lib* hyperbole, as I have since heard no one either in the Administration or out of it upholds, or even attempts to uphold it.

The notion of making our Asiatic foreign policy "credible" by nuclear weapons is entirely different from—and, indeed, more shocking than—the mere advocacy of a limited ABM system. If the new "Nixon doctrine" means that the U.S. will not commit substantial ground troops in Southeast Asia in the future, the President would seem to be proposing that undesirable moves by Communist forces in that area will be met by the threat of nuclear attack. He thus seems to have abandoned our "deterrent" strategy and embraced that of "massive retaliation." (How true it is that the more Republican Administrations change, the more they remain the same!) Furthermore, one wonders how such a threat could be made "credible" in order to discourage a possible Chinese attack against her neighbors, if we cannot even rely—as "Safeguard" proponents affirm—upon our destructive nuclear arsenal to deter a Chinese attack upon the United States, even when China has only a few such weapons.

We have been hearing about the Chinese nuclear threat for several years now. It has become the new club which the military-industrial complex flauntingly wields to win greater and greater appropriations from the Congress. But I question whether the execution of the threat is in any way imminent, and I incline to believe that we do have a considerable time factor in our favor. It still seems to me that it would be suicidal for the Chinese to unloose a few nuclear weapons upon the United States and thus invite retaliatory destruction. This is completely contrary to the common-sense foundation of the theory of deterrence, unless, of course, one accepts the old racist canard that the Chinese—with their "teeming population," "ant-hill existence," etc.—place no value whatever on human life.

So, the ABM defense, instead of being "virtually infallible," turns out to be fallibly virtual—that is, in theory illogical, and in practice ineffective. One might go so far as to suggest that the proposed "Safeguard" against this hypothetical Chinese threat may be merely another camel-nose tactic for the full ABM deployment which the military-industrial complex so ardently desires. Of course, this is not the motive of all its advocates who can be found in both parties and in all segments of the parties—as of course is equally true of ABM opponents. For myself, unless our security requires it—and ABM was surely not required—I see no reason for feeding the flames of international hostility by the continued piling of weapons system on top of weapons system. And at such a cost!

Domestic needs, which have been unmet for years, cry out for solution. Unfortunately, to President Nixon a dollar spent on educating our children is highly inflationary, while ten dollars spent for useless and potentially dangerous weapons is, somehow, not inflationary.

But the most serious implication of any ABM deployment is its effect upon the prospects for successful conclusion of an agreement at the Strategic Arms Limitation Talks or at whatever subsequent arms-control negotiations may ensue. The implications will be equally grave whether ultimately a "thick" or "thin" ABM system is created. For the level of ABM defenses which may be successfully negotiated at the SALT, or other similar such conferences, might well determine the limitations on offensive and defensive strategic weapons that are subject to mutual agreement. The more uncertainty aroused by the ABM deployment, the greater will be the insistence both within the U.S. and within the U.S.S.R. for "damage-limiting" defensive deployment. And the more defensive deployment, the more offensive deployment will be necessary to retain either "balance" or "superiority" in nuclear arms.

Now is the time to call a halt to this seemingly endless escalation. More than a year ago former Secretary of Defense Clark Clifford observed: "The hard fact is that we may never again expect to be in as favorable a position as we now enjoy for entry into talks about a freeze in strategic nuclear armaments. Technological developments may well make any arms limitation agreement more difficult to develop and enforce a year from now, or six months from now, than it is today." That "today" has long since passed.

Of course, there are still some people, I am sorry to say, both in and out of government, who feel that "it is impossible to do business with the Russians" on any basis. And they are so distrustful of our ability to protect our own interests in negotiations that they feel it best not even to enter into preliminary discussions. This is both ridiculous and dangerous—for us and for the rest of the world. As William C. Foster, former chairman of our Arms Control and Disarmament Agency, wrote in *Foreign Affairs* (April, 1969): "Many people have the impression that dealing with the Soviets is like dealing with creatures from another planet. That has not been the experience of this observer. On the whole they have shown much the same personal reactions as Westerners. Moreover, they respect candor about basic conditions which cannot be waived in a negotiation—just as they respect those who keep their confidences."

This in general reflects my own experience with Soviet negotiators—with whom I have had a good deal of contact both at the U.N. and as Senate delegate-advisor to various Geneva conferences on nuclear weapons—and leads to my belief that the political leaders of this country would do well not to abet and exploit the popular American apprehensions about being "unable to do business with the Russians." This call to enlightened leadership has not been well-heeded, if at all heard, by some spokesmen for Mr. Nixon.

There is apprehension and distrust on both sides of what is becoming an ever thinner, though still existent, iron curtain. Because of this mutual distrust, both nations have habitually kept ready or in development almost every new weapon its strategists, whether military or civilian, want to test and deploy. There can never be a "sufficiency" to use President Nixon's expression, for these strategists—not from here to doomsday, which quite simply is where we have been heading. These are the people whose spokesman used to be Senator, then candidate, Goldwater: "We should, I believe, announce in no uncertain terms that we are *against* disarmament. We are *against* it because we need our armaments—all of those we presently have, and more" (original italics).

Any agreement with the Soviets—on arms limitations or on anything else—should be one that is capable of verification. This was a major reason that the Nuclear Test Ban treaty, as I insisted at the time, should not include underground tests. Neither side was sure that a violation by the other would go undetected. But we can detect an atmospheric test, or one under water, or in space.

Any agreement with the Soviets must serve and protect our national interests; similarly, we cannot expect them to agree to anything that fails to safeguard what they regard as their vital concerns. But there are areas in which there is a mutuality of interest. Surely both we and they share an interest in halting dangerous and costly escalation of the nuclear arms race, under conditions by which neither side would gain an advantage. In fact, never in history have there been two nations with a greater mutuality of interest, in that never have two nations had as much to lose from all-out war, or from a continued drain on those national resources that might well be applied to constructive purposes.

Agreement can come only when there is relative parity. We have a sort of parity now in the sense that each side can destroy the other several times over. Those who believe that ABM, or the next round, or the next, will place us in such a strong position that we could, and would, be able to engage in nuclear blackmail to compel submission of our adversaries misread the history of the nuclear arms race and of human nature as well.

A brief chronicle of our race to the top of the nuclear volcano will support my sharply critical judgment above. In 1961 the Soviets had but a small number of ICBM's, but the United States, not believing that a small number would "satisfy the Russians" and feeling that we might be overtaken, undertook a gigantic expansion of the Minuteman and Polaris forces. We ended up with many more weapons than were needed to destroy Russia several times over. Then the Soviets responded to our increased efforts by intensifying their own ICBM program and building their own nuclear submarine fleet. The age of overkill was upon us!

At present, both sides are working on some form of multiple independently targetable re-entry vehicle. This represents a uniquely dangerous type of escalation since it undermines our retaliatory strategy by not allowing either side any certitude about how many weapons may in fact be deployed. In turn, each side must, therefore, assume that each missile installation is equipped with the maximum number of warheads. Both psychologically and factually, this is a terrifying situation since either side may regard itself as being in a position to launch a successful "first strike." The Soviets now seem to be developing a "Fractional Orbital Bombardment System" which theoretically would be almost impossible to detect and destroy, since the assault weapons may come in at a low level, at a relatively flat angle. Conceivably, such a system would threaten our bomber fleet on the ground. Thus, again, a "first strike" capability could be said to be in the process of development. And, of course, we will react in kind. —*Of course*: but why always "of course"? Is it not time that this game of technological leapfrog was brought to an end? It adds nothing to the security of anyone elsewhere in the world, and it destroys the possibility of "domestic tranquility" at home by reason of its astronomical costs.

And since I am here seeking to sketch a "people's politics," a politics which is responsive to the needs of the people, it is to this last point of exorbitant expense that I would briefly advert before concluding. Let us consider but two brief examples. In 1960 Air Force officials estimated that the cost of developing and deploying an ICBM system would be about $3.3 million per missile. By the time the Minuteman was ready for deployment in 1965, the cost had leaped to almost $8.5 million per missile. We now have more than 950 such missiles. Similarly, two years ago the Defense Department projected estimates of roughly $5 billion for a "very light" ABM system. But it began to appear almost immediately that the cost of even this so-called "starter" system would run closer to $10 billion or even more—it is always difficult to get official figures, though some outside experts have published some really frightening cost estimates. Now, just by way of simple comparison, for $10 billion we could build some 600,000 family housing units which are urgently needed.

The domestic needs of our society and the peace of the whole world are too great for any nation to squander its riches on destructive weapons or on futile efforts to protect against such weapons. The only true protection against nuclear exchange is the prevention of that exchange. Once it has started, both sides have lost: all has been lost.

The search for some formula to bring nuclear weapons under control has been an urgent task of four administrations, beginning with President Eisenhower. The task remains. Whether it will be successfully prosecuted by the present Administration is still uncertain. The ABM advocacy, the continuing troglodytic utterances of Mr. Agnew, the President's own opposition to the Non-Proliferation Treaty as a candidate—though later endorsing it—all this makes the future problematic.

Still one must have faith in the future, faith not in patrician groups or elites—a given government, the military, the scientific community, etc.—but in the people. Nixon won the first round with his ABM proposal. He will lose the second or the third. The American people are too aware of their humanity, of their needs which are common to all peoples. The sentiment for a reordering of priorities runs very deep in the people of this nation. And so, too, does common sense, that common sense which no longer blindly trusts the words of the experts, of the professional planners, of the "new mandarins," who have led us into this valley of the shadow.

4.

Energy and Environment

Man, the most adaptable of animals, has been at all times and in all places the greatest despoiler of nature. He wants quick and often drastic changes in his environment. The animal is in a hurry, and cannot wait for genetic adjustments within himself to conform to his surroundings; so he forces his surroundings into the pattern of his transitory wants. Before the technological revolution and in a less crowded past, man could develop, despoil, destroy, and move on—witness the Indian-burned areas of woodlands noted by the earliest European settlers in America, or our more recently denuded and eroded hillsides. But today the world is becoming more and more a closed, interlocked system ecologically as well as economically. Any resource development, any use of natural and synthetic products, and any effort for conservation must now be carried forward with a view to its effect on each element in the entire system.

This organic interrelation of all the elements has certainly been blatantly ignored in many manufacturing and industrial processes. And it is easy for the general public, only recently aroused to the problem, to stridently accuse greedy land developers, arrogant manufacturers, predatory fishermen, etc., of wasting our resources, poisoning our atmosphere, and in general abusing the human habitat. All this is easy, and all this is entirely proper: the public should be enraged. But the danger is that, as with all intensely motivated crusades, zeal may evolve into fanaticism, righteousness into arrogance.

I plead therefore for balance, for an awareness of the harmony that must prevail among these three elements—*resource development*, *use*, and *conservation*—if our social order is not to degenerate into chaos. Let it be candidly admitted that the unchecked abuse of our natural resources is one of the greatest evils that has afflicted industrialized, technological man. But it is axiomatic that the prevalence of abuse should not preclude rightful use.

"Ecology" is now a household word, but many of those who use it do not seem aware of the fact that by definition ecology is tied to economics, that man's *well-being* is tied to his *being*; that although preservation of an unsullied crystal stream, a purer atmosphere, a virgin tract of forest, or an unblemished landscape are noble goals, they are not the noblest: the noblest is to provide man with the basic stuff of his existence: food, and housing, and meaningful work. Before we can recreate we must create.

Unquestionably man lives poorly if "by bread alone." He needs a large infusion of beauty, serenity, spaciousness, all of which can best be imparted by unspoiled natural surroundings, clear air, clean water, forests, and plains. This must be borne in mind when we appropriate natural resources to our own use if our lives are not to be "solitary, nasty, brutish." On the other hand, the purely utilitarian aspects of resource development must be given due consideration if Hobbes' other adjectives, "poor" and "short," are not to come into play through widespread hunger, disease, and insufficient protection against the elements.

Our fundamental resource is the land and its products, nutriments, and minerals, for we must base most of our economic existence on the food, fiber, and industrial raw materials we get from it, and we must base most of our leisure existence on its wealth of space and varied topography. Despite the sometimes shrill warnings we hear today with increasing frequency, we are in no danger of exhausting our usable land for the growing of food and fiber. Less than 50 per cent of the acreage in the United States which is suitable, or which could be made suitable through irrigation or drainage, for crop land is now being used. The remainder is in pasture or forests. In fact, crop acreage is expected to decrease between now and 1980, after which time agricultural requirements will probably require a slight increase in land usage. Moreover, fifty years from now, crops and grazing space will require about the same acreage as now, though it will produce enough food and fiber for a population two and a half times as large as our present one. I cite these few statistics to show that we are in no immediate danger of running out of usable land. It should be remembered that the core of our "farm problem" is overproduction.

As the principal Senate sponsor of the Interstate Highway System, I am perhaps overly sensitive to loose talk about the pace of highway construction being so fast that we are either in danger of taking too much farm land out of production or of carving up the landscape with too many concrete and asphalt monstrosities. All of this is utter nonsense. Indeed, it is high time we began to plan for the expansion of the Interstate System. We need more direct routes, more economical, and more safe highway transportation—and I would emphasize this matter of safety. Construction of the 41,000 miles of Interstate Highways already authorized will be completed within a few years. Since there is considerable lead-time required for planning and engineering work, early Congressional action to expand this system is imperative.

Let me point out at this juncture a peculiar self-contradiction among some of our newly fledged militant conservationists who decry the extension of our federal highway system, but who at the same time are the first to take advantage of it when, in a two-or-three-week vacation period and on a limited budget, they want to go with their families to visit distant relatives or to enjoy the facilities of one of our far-flung national parks. Here, as always, it should be remembered that we must maintain a balance among conflicting needs. Preservation of the beauty of our landscape is a priority, but travel and commerce may frequently override such otherwise legitimate aesthetic concerns. Once again, the issue is a people's politics for the future. The vast majority of our lower economic groups travel neither by air nor by rail; they travel by bus or private car on our federal highways. One need only visit any large airport terminal to realize the truth of this statement.

But I would agree with those critics of our Interstate System who are disturbed by the immense commercial advertisements that now in many places clutter up its environs. It had been anticipated by those of us who strove to have these new roads developed that due consideration would be given to this aesthetic element. In the over-all this has been done; but there was so much planning to be concerned with initially that we neglected to include adequate billboard control provisions. Several determined efforts to correct this oversight have been made during the past few years, but the present provisions which merely "encourage" the states to take action are unsatisfactory. Hopefully something more adequate will be worked out when the system is extended.

Today, I suppose clean water is receiving as much attention as any other aspect of our environment—as well it should. Whether it is receiving sufficiently *effective* attention is open to argument. Not only is it past time for us to clean up our streams and lakes, we must also begin giving more consideration to future needs for water. It is most unlikely that we will run out of water on a nationwide basis; it *is* likely—if it has not already happened—that we will run out of the right kind of water in many sections of the country.

According to a recent report of the Water Resources Council, we need to spend $20 billion during the next four or five years on capital outlays for improved waste treatment, for building sanitary sewers, for separating sanitary from storm sewerage, and for water cooling to cut down on thermal pollution. Of course, this amount of money would not now be necessary if we had not allowed a backlog of tasks to accumulate. We must now redeem the failures of the past, and I do not detect any real sense of urgency on the part of the Administration to undertake this kind of effort. Most of the money for this work must come from the federal government, but Congress will have difficulty appropriating sufficiently for it in the face of Administration hostility, reluctance, or indifference.

As to our total water supply, future prospects are not bleak, but neither are they so bright as to warrant waste and neglect. In the conterminous United States—the forty-eight states—natural water runoff amounts to about 1200 billion gallons per day. We consume only some 80 billion gallons, although we withdraw from streams and reservoirs and underground about 270 billion gallons per day. Much of this withdrawal is returned to the rivers, and so long as it is neither unclean nor overheated, it can be used again downstream. This is important, and will become doubly so in about fifty years when withdrawals are expected to amount to about 1400 billion gallons per day—more than the natural runoff. We must improve our water use throughout the nation, but more particlarly in the Southwest where water is always in short supply. Water can be recycled, salt or brackish water can be used for some purposes, and better purification of industrial wastes can be accomplished. This too will require the appropriation of money—great sums of money which may not be forthcoming until we can loose the millstone of Vietnam from around our neck. But at least now we have legislative precedent for that preservation of our water supply which is demanded on economic, health, and aesthetic grounds. The Water Quality Act of 1965 and the Water Resources Planning Act of the same year were landmarks of legislation in this field.

One of our great water reclamation and usage projects has been the Tennessee Valley Authority. I do not introduce this subject out of any kind of naïve local pride, nor even because I am so familiar with its operations, but simply because of the vast benefits TVA has brought both to the residents of the Valley and to the entire country. The effectiveness of its management and the dedication of its employees have made the whole nation its debtors. And speaking more personally, I can now see that TVA has had much to do with molding my own views on government's role in economic and social development generally.

Both because the Tennessee Valley Authority is a model of how the powers of government can be used positively for the benefit of all the people, and because it has been a test case in the perennial conflict between the advocates of refurbished *laissez-faire* capitalism and the advocates of government-regulated free enterprise—because of both of these reasons, it is desirable that we examine the history of TVA more fully.

The Tennessee Valley Authority was organized by Congress in 1933 as a separate but wholly owned government corporation. For years some such move had been debated, and much of the debate had centered around the disposition of Muscle Shoals Dam on the Tennessee River in northern Alabama. This Dam had been erected during World War I to provide nitrates needed for explosives. It was a well-built and well-planned structure, and the complex included powerhouses and a chemical plant. It had cost $158 million, a sizable amount of money in those days. During the Republican twenties, the occupants of the White House seemed intent on either giving away this asset or at least on preventing its being used for any larger public purpose. Congress debated for years and finally, in 1928, voted to keep the facility under government ownership, sell the power generated to consumers, and use the proceeds from power sales to improve and lower the cost of fertilizers produced by the chemical plant. Needless to say, this did not receive Presidential approval; both Coolidge and Hoover were opposed to the federal operation of such a facility, even though it was obvious that such operation would be in the public interest. It was only when the Democrats were in control of both Congress and the Executive that the Muscle Shoals question was settled, and the Tennessee Valley Authority began to contribute to the economic, social, and environmental rejuvenation of the seven-state region—an area larger than New England.

I followed TVA activities with great interest, particularly after I became Commissioner of Labor for Tennessee and came to know more about state-wide and area-wide problems. The more I became aware of the crucial economic and social issues plaguing the region—issues which were not then being satisfactorily resolved—the more firmly convinced I was that government cannot leave the development of its natural resources to self-serving industrial opportunists. I welcomed TVA's progress in getting cheap electric power to the people who needed it in their homes—"cheap" both through rural electrification and through the pressure of public opinion TVA exerted on the privately owned power companies in the surrounding area. After all, it was no longer necessary to argue purely from a theoretical standpoint that electricity could be made available to everyone at moderate rates. TVA was proving by doing.

Before long, the farms in the valley began to show the effects of better and cheaper fertilizer, of erosion control, of reforestation. Concomitantly, industry began to move in, and this not merely in response to cheap power, but to the availability of plentiful supplies of power, to better water transportation, to increased local demand, to a labor force improved by healthier working conditions, better education, and expanded recreation areas.

From a purely monetary standpoint, all the country has benefited from TVA, for the government not only receives a regular return on its investment, it also is being repaid for earlier appropriations for TVA's power purposes. Last year TVA paid $68.1 million into the U.S. Treasury. And in addition, TVA and its distributors paid to local and state governments, in lieu of the taxes privately owned utilities might have paid, $37.4 million. No funds have been appropriated by Congress for the power program since 1959 and very few since 1953. This program is self-supporting and self-liquidating—a vastly profitable government investment.

It has been one of the nation's most successful experiments in the kind of balanced ecological development I have been advocating throughout this chapter: it improved farm land, fostered industrialization, conserved resources, created new jobs, and opened up new recreational facilities. *But* it was an experiment which the first Republican Administration since the time of Hoover—and I say this in no mere partisan sense—was intent on dismembering or selling.

In the election campaign of 1952 I was elected to the Senate, but Adlai Stevenson—victim of General Eisenhower's popularity—was defeated. TVA was one of the issues that year, and the General, having been well-coached, was unequivocal in his support of it. On October 15, he told his audience, "Certainly there will be no disposition on my part to impair the effective working of TVA." Just before the election on November 2, a telegram from President Eisenhower was highlighted in the Tennessee press.

> "TVA has served well both agricultural and industrial interests of this region. Rumors are being maliciously spread in TVA areas that I propose not only to decrease the efficiency of the operation but to abandon it, which is grossly untrue and utterly false. If I am elected President, TVA will be operated and maintained at maximum efficiency. I have a keen appreciation of what it has done and what it will be able to continue to do in the future. Under the new administration TVA will continue to serve and promote the prosperity of this great section of the United States."

Yet not long after Eisenhower's inauguration I began to hear rumors which could not be dismissed as "grossly untrue and utterly false." In fact, after a trip on the Eisenhower plane Senator Lyndon Johnson, then Democratic leader of the Senate, told me of a conversation that he had inadvertently overheard during which President Eisenhower said, "We will sell the **** **** thing." This provoked me, and while I could not at the time publicly relate what

Senator Johnson had told me, I did alert a number of key people in the entire seven-state area about it.

Within less than six months President Eisenhower eliminated from the new budget funds for the construction of badly needed generating facilities in the western portion of "that great section of the United States" served by TVA. Then combining his expert knowledge of socio-economics with his really genuine penchant for reducing the most complex problems to slogans, the President began to associate TVA with "creeping socialism"—augmented by a later reference to the provision of "cheap power" by TVA as "this curious thing in socialist theory. . . ." Curiouser and curiouser! The one-time general's chosen sapper (I use the term, naturally, as an appropriate military metaphor), one A. H. Wenzell, an employee of the First Boston Corporation, later disagreed with his chief's "creeping socialism," and opined instead: "I would call it galloping socialism."

Edgar H. Dixon and Eugene A. Yates were corporate executives of Middle South Utilities, Inc., and the Southern Company, large utility combines in the Mid-South area. Though well-known in corporate circles, they were relatively obscure insofar as the general public was concerned. But in the mid-1950s their names were to become household words.

What came to be called the Dixon-Yates controversy began to take preliminary shape on May 11, 1953, when George Woods, Chairman of the First Boston Corporation, came to Washington to see Joseph M. Dodge, Director of the Bureau of the Budget. Mr. Woods wanted to help in getting the government out of business—never, of course, with any thought that his own company might gain from the process. So, Mr. Woods deputed Mr. Wenzell as First Boston's man in Washington—at government expense. Mr. Wenzell set about his work in such an aura of secrecy that

Bureau of the Budget people were cautioned not to let anyone know of his presence—particularly anyone connected with TVA. By September 3, 1953, Wenzell had completed his report and a copy was delivered to the President by the Director of the Bureau. A copy was also sent to former President Herbert Hoover whose "task force" report on TVA followed the Wenzell line closely: sell TVA's power and fertilizer facilities to private investors.

The Dixon-Yates strategy began to take more specific form. But although it involved TVA and the people of Memphis most directly, neither officials of the city nor of the Authority were consulted. Instead, Admiral Lewis L. Strauss, Chairman of the Atomic Energy Commission, together with Joseph Dodge, Director of the Bureau of the Budget, worked out the specific contents and procedures of the Dixon-Yates contract. The financial agent in the transaction was to be the same Messrs. Woods' and Wenzell's omnipresent First Boston Corporation. In those high Republican circles economic virtue was its own reward.

There are still some who would defend Dixon-Yates. There are some who simply cannot understand the gravity of this kind of pillage of a vital regional facility or of any other publicly owned resource. Those who would rob the people of their public property do not openly proclaim their intentions from the rooftops. They set about it shrewdly, with subtle orchestration by Madison Avenue, and approach their victim without forewarning him. Fortunately a few of us had been alerted (the late Senator Estes Kefauver, former Senator Lister Hill, Senator John Sherman Cooper) and we struggled against the insidious attackers who were well-armed with power, wealth—and slogans. But it was only the outraged cry of the public, when the machinations of some of the financial people were revealed, that finally laid this scheme to rest.

We will shortly be faced with another attempt to promote a massive "sale" of the property of the people, held in trust for them by their government. This time the consequences could be immeasurably graver—frightening from some points of view. I refer to a proposal made by President Nixon for the sale of our huge nuclear facilities, particularly the gaseous diffusion plants at Oak Ridge, Paducah, and Portsmouth. Here again, as in Dixon-Yates, some of the background must be sketched if the problem is to be understood in its fullest dimension. And, again, we have a situation in which there is a collision between the various elements that constitute a viable socio-economic equilibrium: basic needs *v.* controllable pollution.

Although exhaust fumes from transport vehicles—cars, trucks, jet airplanes, diesel-electric railway engines, etc.—seem to be presently the major polluter of our atmosphere, some conservation groups have concentrated on electric power plants, with particular emphasis on nuclear-fueled generating plants. The dilemma is obvious: on the one hand is the inescapable fact that all power plants cause pollution; on the other hand is the absolute need of all the people for more and cheaper electricity. Let us examine this latter factor first. According to present estimates, the demand for electric power by 1980 will be 150 per cent of the 1965 level. And by the year 2000, which is now a short generation away, the United States will require two and one half times as much electricity as it did in 1965. Thus during the immediate, short-term planning period 1974-80 we must create more new generating capacity than the total capacity now in being. For geographic and logistic reasons a great many of the new plants must be nuclear fueled.

Now, as I have mentioned, all power plants cause pollution—particulate, thermal, or radiation. One could suggest, and some of the more extreme conservation groups have in fact suggested, that pollution be cut back by reducing the demand for power. This is clearly an unrealistic solution, and how one would go about implementing it has never been spelled out. With accelerating population growth and increased crowding of our cities and suburban areas, we will require greater and greater quantities of electric power if the general quality of our lives is not to retrogress. The choice is really not power or pollution, but control of pollution by cleaner power generators.

Our fossil-fueled plants can be improved—improved in efficiency so that more power per ton of coal is produced, and stack emissions reduced. There is also some promising work being done in a completely new area of power generation, MHD (Magnetohydrodynamic), which may effect greater efficiency than the steam turbo-machinery now in use. An efficiency of perhaps ten percentage points higher than is now achieved or achievable with conventional machinery—whether fossil or nuclear fueled—may be attainable by MHD, and this regardless of what primary energy is used. But such a breakthrough is far in the future unless research and developmental work is drastically intensified.

Therefore, for the next decade or two at least, we must increasingly rely on nuclear-fueled electrical generation. At present we are still proceeding with relatively primitive reactor concepts. Instead of cutting back on expenditures for studies with breeder reactors, with molten salt reactors, with liquid metal reactors, we should be increasing this program to resolve the problem both of pollution and of fuel needs. That means that for the current decade we simply must have increasingly large supplies of enriched uranium to fuel existing and projected power plants.

This brings us back to our initial topic of government policy and prospective action concerning our present three gaseous diffusion plants. The sole source of enriched uranium in the United States and—so far as any really significant quantities are concerned—outside the Communist sphere, are the government-owned plants at Oak Ridge, Paducah, and Portsmouth. These constitute one of the most important factors in our future economic growth; and, as I shall point out in a moment, they are of great significance for our broad-gauge foreign policy.

President Nixon's proposal that we sell these nuclear fuel plants is really but an extension of the long dark shadow of Dixon-Yates. Both the pretext and the strategy are identical. (Who says there is a "new Nixon"? In economic matters, the new Nixon is just Hoover-Eisenhower.) The excuse for initiating the Dixon-Yates move was to avoid appropriating funds to construct a new TVA power plant; the excuse being used now is to avoid appropriating money to modernize and upgrade these nuclear fuel plants. In Dixon-Yates, the agency most directly concerned, the Tennessee Valley Authority, was by-passed and the scheme was arranged in the White House with the Atomic Energy Commission. Ironically, this time the Atomic Energy Commission, the agency most directly concerned now, has been by-passed. Initially it was not even allowed a seat on the committee which President Nixon secretly convened. Nor was the Joint Congressional Committee on Atomic Energy—which the law requires should be kept informed of such matters—invited to attend these sessions.

Finally on November 10, 1969, the White House routinely issued a low-keyed press release stating that President Nixon proposed that these plants "should be transferred to the private sector, by sale, at such time as various national interests will best be served . . ." These plants, as I told my colleagues in the Senate early in 1970, "are absolutely essential for weapons production as well as for the production of fuel for nuclear reactors used for electric power generation." Nevertheless, notwithstanding the importance of these facilities, a firm decision has apparently been taken by the Administration to sell them. The timing will probably be determined by the results of the fall elections in 1970 which will decide just how the new Congress views the "national interests" which are to "be served" by the government's proposed giveaway of our vital resources.

Whatever may be the timetable, it is important that the American people fully understand the serious implications of this transaction. The impact of such a sale on the national security of the country and the economic welfare of our people would, in my opinion, be most adverse to the public interest. The security issue is perhaps the most important. These plants produce material used in the manufacture of weapons—nuclear weapons. And while it is patent from everything in the preceding chapter that I hope the nuclear arms race can be stopped, our national security could not possibly be furthered by the government's giving up control over these plants which are essential to weapons production. Such a transfer to the private sector would also have a direct bearing on nuclear weapons proliferation if the 33 foreign governments and international bodies, to which we have agreed to furnish enriched uranium for nuclear reactors, were to conclude that U.S. private corporations might not live up to official agreements. It is entirely possible that many of these governments will decide to build their own nuclear enrichment plants.

But even apart from all considerations of foreign policy, the internal economic problems posed by this move are too serious to pass by without the closest scrutiny. These plants cost $2.3 billion to build. Who could buy them, except at a really giveaway price? According to projections, they might not show a profit for several years if they are privately operated, although they provide considerable income now with a large increase forecast about 1980. There are currently some half dozen companies actively involved in the nuclear-reactor business. Perhaps a consortium of these companies would be interested in acquiring the plants in order to supply their own fuel requirements—and to forestall any possible future competition. Such vertical integration—to put it baldly, such a "cartel"—has always been opposed in this country, particularly since we began to try some eighty years or so ago to restore genuine competition to the free enterprise system.

The giant oil companies are in the energy business. They have been busy in recent years buying up the larger and more productive coal companies in order to enhance their position as controllers of fuel sources. Would it promote the health of the economy to give them control over all fuel sources, nuclear fuel included? Even if these three plants were sold to separate owners the problem would not be solved. As the Chairman of the Board of Consolidated Edison recently warned, this would lead to the kind of "homogeneous oligopoly" that would make meaningful competition questionable.

Within a very few years, one-half of our electrical energy will be generated from nuclear fuel. The demand for such fuel, for the enriched uranium these plants supply, will exceed their productive capacity by the year 1980. Immediate appropriations are clearly required to upgrade existing capacity, to prepare for new plants, and to expand existing ones to meet this inevitable increased demand. Yet President Nixon evaded the appropriations issue this year by recommending such a small allocation of funds that it is obvious that he has opted for delay, and looks forward to disposing of the facilities. Similarly, he has side-stepped the responsibility of seeking adequate funds for research and development in pollution control from nuclear-fueled electric power plants.

Radiation emission—an emotional thing since any nuclear device conjures up visions of physiological horrors—must be more closely studied. In my opinion, however, radiation is not now the imminent peril some of the opponents of new power plant locations have depicted it as being. The Atomic Energy Commission, supported by the findings of independent authorities, has established criteria, and these are almost universally being observed. There may be a need for greater restrictions, but this is a matter to be resolved by impartial research, not by the conjuring up of emotional specters.

Thermal pollution constitutes a real danger, a far greater danger with nuclear than with present fossil-fueled generating plants. And this type of pollution simply must be brought under control. But here, too, money will have to be expended—and the present Administration seems not to want to spend required funds for research and development.

Today there is widespread concern over our environment, our quality of life, our resource adequacy, our crowded future. We have pushed back the limits of Malthus' close and dismal horizons, but the common sense of the people has discerned a fact still apparently concealed from many of our political leaders: there are limits to resource waste, to environmental pollution, and to population growth.

"Social organization" (though a dirty word to those whose lexicons contain fearsome definitions of such myths as "creeping socialism") must become a reality. "Social organization" is simply the antidote to unbridled industrial license and to *laissez-faire* human development. Pollution control and resource conservation will require greater restrictions, particularly in crowded areas. We do not get something for nothing either socially or economically. Some price must be paid, and in this instance the price will be the judicious exercise of federal authority. Particularly where air pollution is concerned, supervision cannot be left to local efforts. Not even statewide efforts will suffice, for too many of our cities are located near state lines, and polluted air is no respecter of borders. I hope the start which has been made in implementing the Congress's Air Quality Act can be continued and that we will move on to more comprehensive legislation.

All of us know what the core of the problem is: the polluters simply want maximum profits. Part of their gain would be dissipated if they were forced to install machinery, move to better locations, or alter manufacturing processes in order to alleviate pollution. The problem is just *that* elementary. Many industrialists are still living in the nineteenth century when, for example, a mill owner built his mill on the river front, and workers who could not afford transportation lived in crowded hovels and tenements around the mill, while the owner and his family lived up above on the summit far removed from pollution of air and water. Well, this kind of thing will just not do today. The problem is too big and the social conscience is honed too fine.

Much as it goes against many of our better instincts and emotional habits, I see no way to avoid a greater degree of social discipline over the individual—exercised, it must be emphasized, through persuasion and economic and moral incentives. There may be no such thing as a "critical mass" of people, as there is of uranium; but it does seem to me that where greater density of population occurs tighter social organization must be provided either by government or by other agencies representing the *whole* society. The Administration, ever alert to the foibles and flaws of the poor and dispossessed, has publicly advocated limiting our over-all population growth. But this growth is only truly alarming among the lowest economic levels of our society, and the way to reduce the birth rate on those levels is by better education, improved job opportunities, cheaper housing, etc.—precisely the very same social instruments which tended to reduce birth rates among our new middle class. *And,* one regrets having to say, the very same social instruments that this Administration has done so much to blunt and render useless.

We have come a long way in our thinking about national natural resources since the days of Theodore Roosevelt. In those earlier and simpler times we were concerned, for example, about the disappearance of our forests, and conservationists viewed with alarm the wasteful cutting of trees—and they were right. There is less worry about such things now: there seems to be a plentiful supply of forest land both for timber and for recreational purposes. Our problems of today are of a different quality, a more frightening quality, which may perhaps be best epitomized by the very real prospect that man may so upset the atmosphere, by increasing its carbon dioxide content, that the whole earth's climate will be changed. However distant that dismal prospect may now appear, it is only in the present that it and similar such horrors can be warded off.

5.

Economic and Social Justice

My earliest recollection of the events which directly shaped my political, social, and economic philosophy are the conversations I had with my father sitting around the fire or on the front porch after supper. Reading his newspaper by the light of the kerosene lamp, he would frequently stop to discuss some new development. Often he would refer to William Jennings Bryan, whose earlier achievements as "the Great Commoner" are still cherished in the memory of the people of my state. The Bryan to whom my father referred, and whom I shall cite in these pages, was not the ineffectual Secretary of State under Wilson, nor the pitiful old man of the "monkey trial," but the dynamic young Cross of Gold Populist.

As one who believes there is much merit in this Populist heritage, it has always seemed to me perfectly logical that government should play an active role in the nation's business affairs, and I have never lost faith in the government's ability to guarantee economic justice to all its people. In like manner, I have never understood the attitude of those economic royalists who prate about the impropriety of positive governmental action in the economic arena.

During my formative years, the Harding-Coolidge-Hoover concept of government, utterly negative as it seemed to me, was in the ascendency. For the most part social problems were left to private agencies for solution. But even in those days the hand of government was evident in some economic matters. The trouble was that—certainly in rural Tennessee and in many other states—the federal government was not acting in the best interests of the people. The government's economic policies, particularly in money and banking, made it almost impossible for a hill farmer to pay off the big mortgage which he had assumed during the more prosperous days after the First World War. That the government should play a more intelligent and humane role in economics was brought home to me not by any theoretical study of the discipline, but by the injustice and impoverishment which would inevitably result from any other policy.

Freedom—political freedom, economic freedom—is an imperative, but freedom to starve is not its necessary accompaniment. After 30 years in the Congress, I am more convinced than ever that economic justice is a prerequisite to social justice, and that the former implies considerably more than merely the correction of physical abuse and degradation. We must go far beyond the eradication of acute want if each citizen is to participate fully in the total social and cultural life of his community. In this chapter I will take up economic justice first, and then go on to discuss the larger, though related, social issues.

1.

In the broad sense, the tools that the government can employ in achieving maximum economic justice for the citizen include taxation, expenditure, and money management. The first two of these fields are commonly denominated "fiscal policy"; the third, money management and all that this implies, is generally denominated "monetary policy." Insofar as the work of an individual senator is concerned, the most crucial of all these areas is taxation. This is true not only because of its intrinsic importance, but even more so because of the organization of our government and the rules and traditions of the Congress. All members of the House and Senate participate broadly in the regulation of expenditures. Bills to authorize various public programs go through the appropriate committees and then are fully and freely debated in both houses. As for monetary policy, the Congress does not directly set interest rates or determine the money supply. Though the Constitution provides that Congress "shall coin money and regulate the value therof," this power has been delegated to the President and the U.S. Federal Reserve System.

Tax bills must originate in the House of Representatives; they are written by the Ways and Means Committee. By tradition of long standing, no amendments to tax bills are allowed during House consideration. The bill as written by Ways and Means must be accepted or rejected—an unwise practice, but one that would be very difficult to overturn. I was frustrated in the House of Representatives by this gag rule. I watched tax bills, many of them highly complicated, come out of Ways and Means, go through a *pro forma* House debate, and then be voted on as a package—usually by overwhelming majorities with few questions raised, and no questions raised effectively. For fourteen years as a Congressman I was never able to offer an amendment to a tax bill, though I felt deeply that tax inequity was one of the blatant injustices of our society. One of the reasons I sought election to the Senate was that I might be able to act more effectively in this area.

Individual Senators can and do offer amendments to tax bills, and a senator who is willing to concentrate on such legislation can play a vital role. It seemed to me, furthermore, that it would only be by assignment to the Senate Finance Committee that I could really be effective in implementing my views on tax inequities. But because I was against the percentage depletion allowance for oil, I was opposed by the most effective lobbying influence on Capitol Hill, that of the oil interests. Eventually, after four years, I received the appointment.

I was soon to learn that service on the Committee entails considerable political risk. The general public, by and large, does not concern itself with the details of tax legislation, and any senator, particularly one on the Finance Committee, must be prepared to fight or to support the special-interest groups—which do follow very closely tax proposals affecting them. While I was already generally aware of this, it was quickly impressed on me by the life insurance lobby.

It was my belief that for years the country's life insurance companies had not been taxed fairly. Under a special formula, since 1921, life insurance companies had paid taxes on only a part of their net investment income. They paid no taxes whatsoever on their underwriting gains, and with changing patterns in the industry—with more and more accident and health, credit, industrial, and other low-reserve and speciality lines being written—underwriting gains were more important to many companies than long-term investments. Stockholders of life insurance companies were reaping immense profits while subsidiaries of mutual companies were extending their control into other businesses through loans from bloated reserves. And all the time, the ordinary taxpayer was being pressed harder and harder to provide the government revenues which should have been paid by these prosperous companies.

Early in 1958, the Senate approved once more a special

formula for the taxation of life insurance companies. I served notice that as far as I was concerned there would be no more stop-gap special arrangements, and that life insurance companies should be taxed more in line with the provisions for other businesses. Now, some of our largest life insurance companies are headquartered in Tennessee, which ranks eighth among all the states in this field. It was not long before it was made clear that anyone who wished to challenge me in my first bid for re-election to the Senate in 1958 would be well financed—after all, this legislation involved hundreds of millions of dollars. Unfortunately, the general taxpayer whom I was defending, seemed unaware of the importance of my efforts. In fact, some people were mistakingly convinced by the insurance companies' propaganda that I was working against the best interests of both the policy holders and the agents. Fortunately, the wisdom of the people prevailed, and after my re-election, I was instrumental in securing adoption of a tax law which required that life insurance companies would carry a fairer share of the tax burden.

In working out the first modern federal income tax program, Cordell Hull, then a Congressman, had proceeded on the principle of taxation according to ability to pay. Nowadays few would openly deny the validity of the general principle, though many would apply it very differently. In fact, some would go no further than proportional taxation—and even Adam Smith got that far 200 years ago. My own support has always gone to a more progressive tax structure, that is, one in which those with higher incomes pay a larger proportion of their incomes in taxes. In actuality, considering the total tax burden in the United States—federal, state, and local—the system as a whole is regressive, with the federal tax structure being the least so. But even here thoroughgoing reform is necessary if the erosion of the tax base, through the creation and the widening of loopholes, is not to continue unabated. The federal income tax is by no means as progressive as the rates would indicate, or as "soak the rich" publicity releases, put out by self-serving critics, would lead one to believe.

During my entire service in the Senate until 1961, there was a Republican in the White House; and while I often found myself supporting the Eisenhower Administration against reactionary Republicans, I did not really expect extensive tax reform until we had a Democratic Administration. I looked forward with eagerness, therefore, to the campaign of 1960 and took an exceedingly active part in it. With the election of Senator John Fitzgerald Kennedy, I anticipated new and determined leadership both from him and his Secretary of the Treasury. But my euphoric hope that the day for tax reform had dawned was soon shattered. With disbelief and chagrin, I heard rumors that a Wall Street Republican, Douglas Dillon, was to be the new Secretary of the Treasury. I felt such an appointment would be a tragic mistake, and set about trying to change Kennedy's mind. In a long letter written to him on November 22, 1960, from my farm in Carthage, I pointed out that under the conditions then existing, his "most important selection" in the Cabinet would be that of Secretary of the Treasury. Since that letter summarizes many of my views on tax reform, I want to quote from it extensively here.

> "Progressive economic and monetary policies have always been distinguishing features of successful Democratic administrations. Without proper economic policies, no other policies can be successfully implemented. . . . The first requisite is to raise the general level of revenue. Without this, it appears to me that your administration will be in an economic straitjacket and devoid of the flexibility necessary to use wisely fiscal, tax, and monetary policies in pursuance of proper economic goals."

I went on to specify some of the various tax loopholes which could be closed to accomplish the necessary increases in revenue. Having also heard rumors that a general tax reduction was favored by some purportedly close to the President-elect, I cautioned against such an action. As for monetary policy, I emphasized that a strong President could "require that it be coordinated with fiscal, economic, debt management, foreign, and related policies. . . . It should always be borne in mind that the Federal Reserve System was established to operate the mechanics of the banking system, *not* to formulate national economic policy." I ended this lengthy letter with the following plea:

> "Why, then, should you consider, even for a fleeting moment, for appointment to the key post of Treasury, one whose chief claim to fame is that he has been a member of a team that failed its most important test? This applies not only to Mr. Dillon, who is an affable easy-goer, but to other conservative Republicans who have been mentioned. For such an appointment would be a signal that you had given up the goals of a truly Democratic Administration in domestic affairs, and, consequently, the progress necessary to restore United States position and prestige abroad. It is only by a truly Democratic Administration that we can achieve power equal to today's world challenge.
>
> "The appointment of such a person as Secretary of Treasury would mean, for instance, that glaring tax "loopholes" would not be closed; that fiscal policies, monetary policies, and economic policies would not be very different from the present [Eisenhower] Administration. This would not be your intention, to be sure, but would be the likely consequence.

I hoped that the President-elect would attend to my warning. We had been Congressmen together; Mrs. Gore and I were among the small group present for dinner the night he had met his future wife; he, myself, and Senator John Sherman Cooper had on an anniversary of that event pooled our plans for announcement of our candidacies for the Senate; we had sat on a number of the same Committees; and, at his personal request, I had accepted the chairmanship of a campaign-strategy board made up of William Fulbright, Clark Clifford, Richard Bolling, and Fred Dutton. I expected that all of this would count for something when we were to discuss the matter at his home in Georgetown. After instructing his aides not to interrupt, we settled down to a long and intense talk. He reminded me that he had received less than 51 per cent of the popular vote, and that he did not believe that he could afford to shake the confidence of the international money marts by appointment of a Secretary of the Treasury who would institute traditional Democratic policies. I strongly resisted, reminding him of his own campaign speeches which I had helped to write. It was to no avail. His mind was already made up. Surely, for a new Democratic President, a personal friend whom I had supported at the convention and helped to elect, to turn the Treasury Department over to a Wall Street Republican constituted one of the gravest disappointments of my political life. Ironically enough, President Kennedy appointed the outstanding progressive economist of the nation, John Kenneth Galbraith, as—of all things—Ambassador to India!

Afterwards I pointed out to Secretary Dillon when he came before the Finance Committee on various occasions the lack of any effective action on his part to bring about tax reforms. It came as no surprise to me, therefore, when the Treasury Department began promoting in the Congress major giveaway tax legislation; and by 1963, the Congress was on the verge of passing a massive, regressive tax reduction bill heavily weighted in favor of the wealthy.

Whatever chance I had of defeating this giant tax bonanza, slim at best, terminated with tragic suddenness in Dallas. Lyndon Johnson felt he had to carry out the unfinished Kennedy program, and—despite previously expressed doubts to me as to the advisability of cutting taxes at that time—did so with skill and vigor. Seeing that it was impossible to defeat the tax cut, I sought to mitigate some of its bad effects by altering its form. I therefore attempted to increase the personal tax exemption to $1000 in lieu of the proposed rate reductions. Either would have occasioned about the same revenue loss, but the rate cuts were so unfair to the low and middle income taxpayers that the over-all burden would have been shifted drastically downward on the economic scale. Ironically, though I lost that battle, I finally achieved this same goal in 1969 under a Republican President—though over his opposition—who also favored a rate reduction that would have made our tax system even more regressive.

The personal exemption provision in the tax code, and its neglect since World War II, illustrates as clearly as anything I know the cavalier treatment of the general taxpayer by Congress and successive administrations over the years. It also reflects the consequences of a lack of organized pressure for tax reform on the part of the public.

A personal income tax system should have two main features. First, a sufficient amount of income should be exempt from taxation so that the taxpayer and his family may enjoy a decent basic living allowance. Second, a graduated tax scale should be applied against all income above the exempt amounts. Tax rates should begin at a very low level—1 or 2 per cent on the lowest taxable amounts—and be graduated upward to high rates on large amounts of income.

Our present federal income tax system is deficient in several respects. The personal exemption is still far too low, tax rates begin at too high a level, the rates are not properly graduated, and too much income is by definition of the code non-taxable. Prior to World War II, the personal exemption was high enough to allow at least a subsistence level of living; but during World War II, as the result of over-all inflation and purchasing-power controls, the personal exemption was drastically lowered. In 1940, a family of four had $2800 tax free; during World War II this was reduced to $2000. When post-war adjustments in the tax system were made, the personal exemption was raised to $600 for the taxpayer and each dependent. Though this was inadequate even then, it had remained at that level, notwithstanding an increase of 50 per cent in the cost of living.

Because I regarded this personal tax exemption as a key to tax equity and, therefore, to economic justice, I have made repeated efforts to get the figure increased. The reason most often advanced for rejecting the increase was the loss of revenue which would be entailed. My fellow Senators and Administration spokesmen would invariably intone pious laments over the situation, but would hasten to point out that a loss of revenue could not be afforded *at this time*. Unfortunately, it always seemed to be *this time*.

In 1964 the excuse was not appropriate, for the Administration and the Congress were setting about deliberately to reduce revenues. But, once again, the exemption was not raised. And the lower and middle income groups were crassly ignored in the rush to cut taxes for the rich and for the big corporations, while a low income allowance was passed for the benefit of some of the extremely indigent. Incidentally, it should be noted that if a general tax provision is to receive any substantial support at all, it must benefit *both* the poor and middle income groups. Tax gimmicks which openly shift the burden to the middle-income group will not survive. In this respect, the personal exemption is a much better vehicle for tax relief than are special low-income allowances, since everyone benefits from an increase in the personal exemption.

But in 1969, the political climate had changed. The Democrats in Congress were determined not to let the new Administration capitalize on a tax-reform bill—which, of course, was no great feat, since Republican Administrations are not generally inclined to think in terms of benefiting the average taxpayer. Thus, when the tax-reform bill came over from the House of Representatives it was not difficult to awaken in my colleagues a concern for the "little man," and to fan into a small flame the residual Populism which lies deep in the hearts of all Democrats, even the most conservative ones. So I won a victory—somewhat scaled down, true, but a victory nevertheless. Congress raised the personal exemption to $750 and made provision for a low income allowance as a substitute for reductions most beneficial to high income brackets.

But the most important aspect of this modest achievement was the fact that we had stopped the trend towards the destruction of progressiveness in our federal system, and we had broken the logjam on the personal exemption. The sacrosanct rate, which had acquired such permanence since 1948, was changed.

Unfortunately, though I consider the raising of the personal exemption in 1969 my greatest triumph in tax legislation to date, I could not take wholehearted joy from it because this really was not the time to reduce taxes. As I pointed out during debate on my amendment: "This amendment offers a fundamental choice to the Senate—a choice between types of tax reductions. It may well be that the bill should contain no tax reductions, and I think I might prefer no tax reductions to the type proposed in the Committee bill." Nevertheless, through this small breakthrough, there is ground for hope that the entire system may be further improved: the amount exempt must be further increased; the rates must be more sharply graduated and must begin at a much lower percentage figure; the definition of taxable income must be refined so that it more closely approximates total income.

My satisfaction at securing adoption of the personal exemption increase was also dulled by my being forced to accept a last-minute bit of connivance between the Administration and the Republicans—aided by some Democrats, I am sorry to say—on the Conference Committee. Though the incident is in itself not of major importance, it does serve to illustrate both the complexity of Congressional procedures in the area of tax reform and the unrelenting pressure upon the Congress by any Republican Administration to favor the business community and the wealthy in tax legislation.

As to procedures, it should be noted that when a bill has passed both House and Senate, there are generally some differences in language between the two versions. In that case, the custom is to appoint a Conference Committee to reconcile the differences. For tax bills, the House conferees come from Ways and Means Committee, and Senate conferees are the senior members of the Senate Finance Committee. Generally the version of the legislation agreed upon by the conferees is accepted by both Houses.

Now, it so happened that the Nixon Administration, in its recurring zeal to help those who least need help, had been anxious from the beginning of consideration of this tax bill to cut the rates applicable to higher income groups; and in addition to a generous rate-reduction, the Administration had the effrontery to propose that the marginal rate—the top rate actually paid—on "earned income" be lowered from 70 to 50 per cent. Assistant Secretary of the Treasury Cohen had persuaded the Ways and Means Committee to agree to this provision. Nor was there any opportunity for a member of the House to offer an amendment to strike such stark favoritism to upper income taxpayers from the bill, since the House of Representatives considers tax bills under a closed—gag—rule.

Upon examining the House bill in preparation for the Senate Finance Committee hearings, I found this provision the most odious of many objectionable features of the bill, and I determined to subject it to the closest scrutiny at the Committee's public hearings. As a result, when closed-door discussions on the bill got under way, the first amendment adopted by the Committee was to strike out this tax-rate cut for the rich. That amendment was offered by the chairman, Senator Russell Long, and was adopted *unanimously*. Moreover, during the long and detailed discussion and debate on this bill in the Senate, no suggestion had been made that this provision be restored—nor, of course, did anyone publicly lament its demise.

It did not occur to me when the Joint Conference Committee from both Houses re-examined the bill that serious attempt would be made to restore this inequitable provision I should have been forearmed, however, since I knew the Administration's tax writers had a special interest in this particular provision. I was only fully alerted to the situation when a vote on it was postponed time after time in conference. Since it was so simple and uncomplicated as to require no detailed study, such repeated postponement made me aware of the pressure for its approval.

When we did finally get around to taking action, the chairman of the Conference, Congressman Wilbur Mills, proposed that as part of a compromise package including the increase in the personal exemption, we should restore this provision for cutting the taxes of the most affluent members of our society. This occurred at about two o'clock in the morning of the last night of the Conference when we were nearing the end of consideration of the many, literally hundreds of issues to be settled. Of course, I immediately and vehemently denounced it as representing the crassest form of favoritism.

The discussion between Congressman Mills and me became intense, if not heated. I will not undertake to state his arguments—I don't think he had any really. Secretary Cohen made a vigorous remonstrance to the effect that "these people" [the rich] "spend a lot of time in arranging ingenious devices to avoid high rates." "So, rather than control these 'ingenious devices'," I said, "instead we just give them this preference." I pointed out, for instance, that the chairman of General Motors would receive unneeded tax relief. His compensaion from General Motors in 1968 amounted to about $795,000, and the adoption of this tax cut would benefit him by some $7500 per month—approximately $90,000 per year. All the while, I was struggling as hard as I could to get a personal exemption allowance of just $750 per year for a hard-pressed wage earner so that he could support, educate, and bring up his children in some degree of decency. I told the Conference Committee that this was "unconscionable, unjustified, unneeded, undeserved, inexcusable."

Chairman Mills then suggested that what he really had in mind was a ceiling on the "effective rate" of taxation. Now, there is a vast difference between the "effective rate" and the "marginal rate." The revenue loss is about $200 million a year if the marginal rate on earned income for the rich is dropped to 50 per cent, while the loss—really the amount of money the middle-income taxpayer pays over to the rich

—is about $15 million if a 50 per cent ceiling on the "effective rate" is applied. So I accepted this offer.

The agreement was reached about 2:30 that morning on an ultimate increase in the personal exemption to $750 for each taxpayer and dependent, and on a maximum "effective rate" of 50 per cent on earned income. Chairman Mills announced that the conferees would meet at noon that same day to review agreements and sign the Conference report. I noticed some whispered discussion among a few members of the Committee and Treasury representatives who were sitting in on our deliberations. As we were breaking up, Senator Wallace Bennett of Utah, who in 1971 will be the ranking Republican on the Senate Finance Committee, said to one of the Treasury officials, "Let's meet in my office." After about three hours sleep I attended a Democratic caucus at 10 A.M. I was rather surprised when Senator Long mentioned to me that it might be necessary to "give" the Administration "something" in order to avoid a veto. Some vague reference was made to the 50 per cent ceiling on high salaries. I was thus forewarned that a deal had been made.

When the Conference Committee met at noon, the play quickly unfolded. Chairman Mills indicated his willingness to reopen discussion on this controversial point. Both Senator Long and Senator Bennett opposed my position. I argued as best I could—a breach of our agreement, unfair, unjustified, etc.—but received no support whatsoever. Except for my own vote, the agreement to adopt the "marginal rate" reduction was unanimous. I believe ultimately this unfair provision will be repealed, but it is always easier to put loopholes into the law than to take them out.

Republicans are very diligent in engineering this kind of gross favoritism, and I suppose such diligence is rewarded by large campaign contributions which, unfortunately, may only render their recipients more indebted to the moneyed interests. I have struggled against this kind of abuse, but I have had to pay for it politically. Campaign money literally floods into my state against me.

Though the tax-reform bill enacted into law in 1969 did represent substantial progress towards tax reform, it did not touch on all areas, nor did it deal adequately with the areas it considered. First, it did not come to grips with the issue of tax exemption afforded the interest on local government bonds. From the standpoint of federal policy alone, this exemption is not justifiable, but the local governmental units have come to rely upon it. Before this can be substantially changed, some mechanism must be found by which states and local governments can be assured of an opportunity to raise needed capital funds at reasonable interest rates. This could be done through direct federal interest rate subsidy, or through a federal guarantee, or possibly through a special arrangement whereby the federal government would make the funds available directly to states and local governments and, in turn, sell federal government bonds to obtain the proceeds. Second, tax treatment of capital gains must be brought more closely into line with the treatment of ordinary income. The 1968 Treasury study showed that the greatest single factor preventing our federal tax system from being sufficiently progressive is the favored treatment now accorded to capital gains. Third, taxation of various components of corporate executive compensation needs a thorough overhaul. This is particularly true with respect to various kinds of deferred compensation. Fourth, charitable contributions and the status of foundations need to be more closely scrutinized and subject to greater restrictions. Fifth, wealthy individuals are still able to take too many unjustified tax "losses," for example through farming operations which are not related to their chief occupations. To the improvement of these and other areas of our tax structure, I shall continue to devote my attention and my energy.

I turn now from fiscal policy to monetary policy.

As old as money is the conflict between debtor and creditor. Creditor groups have always pressed for tight money —"dear" money, it used to be called—so that fixed dollar investments, debts, would be paid back in dollars having no less, and preferably more purchasing power than the dollars originally loaned or invested. From the point of view of the creditors, the higher the interest rate, the better. Debtors, on the other hand, have always been hard-pressed to obtain any kind of currency with which to repay their obligations. This was particularly true in earlier times when our economy was largely agrarian and we had no real national banking system.

With the development of a national banking system, and subsequently with the establishment of the Federal Reserve System, the necessary machinery to supply funds when and where needed was provided. This was intended to be the solution to the old-fashioned "panic," when with disappointing regularity the supply of funds would dry up, and the "shake-out"—so much admired by the "robber barons" —brought business to a standstill.

During the past 15 years or so, the Federal Reserve System, under the chairmanship of William McChesney Martin, could and should have taken care of our monetary and banking problems. Unfortunately it seemed to be operating under an economic philosophy of tight money and high-interest rates and under an administration which neglected the machinery available to it. Of course, Mr. Martin and the other bankers and Wall Street operators who have dominated the Federal Reserve System cannot be held entirely to blame for this misuse of monetary policy. The responsibility for setting broad economic guidelines has rested with the President and the Congress; and as I have noted above, it was never intended that the Federal Reserve should establish national economic policy. Unfortunately, the President and the Congress have more often than not evaded their individual and collective responsibilities and have allowed the Federal Researve to act as if it were by law, as it has been in fact, independent of the United States government. And both the Administration and some Congressional leaders have never ceased to invoke the so-called "independence" of the Federal Reserve as though it were an inviolable charter. But that independence is to be exercised *within* the framework of our total government—there can be no such thing as independence *of* the federal government.

There has been a constant movement upward of interest rates since the Korean War, and a level has been reached in 1970 which is positively dangerous to the continued growth of our credit-based economy. All too often, it has seemed to me, such coordination as we have had between the Federal Reserve and the Administration in power has been aimed almost exclusively at inflation control. Somehow, the idea has been generated and spread that if we can but hold the price line all other desirable economic objectives of government—economic justice, if you will—will automatically result. This is patent nonsense. The control of inflation is highly desirable, but we cannot neglect adequate growth or the proper distribution of goods, wealth, and income among our people. Tight money and high-interest rates can indeed bring economic activity to a halt. But under the conditions of partially administered prices prevailing in our economy, even this will not bring about a price reduction to any given earlier level. It can but slow down the rate of advance of price increases, and at the expense of a hurtful crippling of the total economy.

We have seen repeated misapplications of monetary policy during the last 20 years. We have witnessed mistakes in judgment and misinterpretation of the economic indicators. We have gone through several periods when the timing of changes in monetary policy was extremely poor. Indeed, we have seen so many errors in the efforts of the Federal Reserve to execute a flexible monetary policy that some economists have despaired, and have called for a constant growth in the supply of money in order that there may be fewer disruptions.

Today, interest rates are at historically high levels. But a comparison of present rates with rates of 100 years ago does not spell out by half the dangers and difficulties of the present situation. In a credit-based economy, as ours now is, the more consumers must pay in carrying charges the more they will demand in wage increases. Thus, tight money and high-interest rates become self-defeating as economic regulators in today's market place. Since 1950, interest income has risen more than sixfold, and consumers pay a large part of this unhealthy increase. In 1969, they paid over $15 billion in interest charges. The proportion of disposable personal income paid out in interest doubled between 1950 and 1969. Such greatly increased interest costs add to the pressures for increased income, especially wage demands, and thus contribute directly to the rising cost of living.

But, from the standpoint of economic justice, perhaps the worst thing one can say about tight money and high-interest rates is that they cause disproportionate hardships. This is particularly true when taxes fall short of expenditures in prosperous times, and monetary policy is the only instrument for battling inflation. Housing and its associated industries, along with newly established, small, and weak businesses suffer most of all. Local governments cannot sell bonds and therefore must delay needed construction of such things as schools, sewage treatment plants, and transportation improvements.

Tax equity and correct monetary policy will go far towards keeping the economy healthy and establishing economic justice. But this is by no means enough. In order to achieve a decent standard of living for all our people, more positive action will be needed. Proper programs involving government expenditures must be initiated and implemented. For many people who through background, education, and early experience are well equipped to fight their own battles in our impersonal, individualistic, cybernetic, jungle economy, it is totally inconceivable that some of their fellow citizens are simply not qualified to cope successfully with the day-to-day problems of economic survival. For many of this latter group, it is not enough simply to remove barriers; they must be actively assisted across the threshold separating poverty and plenty. Still others—the sick and the handicapped—must be supported by society on a continuing and regularized basis—and in our affluent society, they should be afforded adequate support without having to undergo any kind of personal degradation.

As a former teacher and as a county superintendent of schools, I have always had great faith in the efficacy of education and training—training for adaptation to the total environment. And so I support federal aid to education, as well as the kind of job retraining programs which are necessary if we are to avoid gross waste of potentially productive effort. Those who cannot be properly housed in high profit, private-enterprise housing must be housed through government programs. Such programs as we now have are deficient because in part they are geared primarily to the enrichment of the real-estate promoter, with the poverty-line tenant being given scant attention. Our free-wheeling, free-enterprise philosophy in this area must be radically amended. The tenant must receive first consideration. The real-estate promoter can enrich himself in the lush private sector. He does not need government subsidies, given liberal credit and interest-rate policies.

Welfare programs of some sort for those who cannot support themselves at a decent level must be continued. Nothing cures poverty like money. There are presently pending several valuable proposals in this area—including President Nixon's—and one can only hope that the Congress will be receptive to the best of them.

Most of our people genuinely want to contribute to society and to the well-being of themselves and their families. But all too often, suitable employment, in terms both of pay and personal satisfaction, is simply not available. Such jobs are beyond the reach of millions of our people. It is my firm conviction that any truly contemporary government worthy of that title is obliged to see that decent work and decent working conditions are accessible to all citizens. Congress recognized this fact in the Employment Act of 1946; but recognition is not tantamount to implementation. Social and economic conditions must be created which are conducive to the growth of the private sector if such jobs are to be provided. Furthermore, if the profit-making segment of the economy does not produce the necessary jobs, the government itself must be the employer—the employer of last resort, true, but the employer nevertheless.

2.

During the past several years, while we have been demonstrating to the world our skill in achieving spectacular technological breakthroughs, we have been undergoing the throes and dislocations of the greatest social revolution of the twentieth century. It is hardly surprising that the pursuit of this noble goal should have been fraught with misunderstanding and bitterness. The creation of even the most grandiose technological schemes demands only the organization of material resources; the social revolution this nation has been pursuing requires a much more profound, and therefore much more unpredictable, spiritual effort.

Perhaps we did not understand the strength of our own rising expectations; perhaps we moved too slowly in meeting needs before they erupted into passionate demands; perhaps we have expected too much of government—at all levels, but particularly the federal government—as the arbiter of social justice and the instrument for social reform. Possibly other agencies of our society, particularly the churches, should have been more vigorously enlisted in this cause. Nevertheless, though there are limits in a free society to what government can do, or even to what government should attempt, it is a fact that the great forward steps in social betterment have come largely through governmental action and leadership. But such action and leadership must of necessity be rooted in popular sentiment and interest, and meet the test of national public acceptance. Consent of the governed is at the heart of our system.

The surging demand for social justice, for wider and more equitable distribution of the fruits of our society, grew out of the hardships and upheaval of the depression period and swept irresistibly through the decades of the 1930's and 1940's. There was a period of relative torpor during the Eisenhower years, but again after the election of Kennedy the movement accelerated and reached its highest peak in the social legislation of the Johnson Administration.

The eye of this storm has moved about, retreating, advancing, never taking a straight course. Nor is it clear whether the storm we are now in is a new one or just a continuation of the old, a hurricane following the brief calm mercifully permitted us. We progressed, but not without retrogression; nor will a straight line of progress ever be discernible. At best, mankind has moved along a sine curve on a slightly ascending axis. Since we must be concerned with practical political problems and not with utopian dreams (though the utopian dream may often be a strong motive for progress), one of our endless concerns must be to secure solid gains on the upswing which will not be lost in a period of reaction, or repression, which inevitably follows. Today we stand on a thin border line between stagnation and explosion. The racial question, which is our most persistent social issue, seems about to be shunted aside through what is euphemistically termed "benign neglect" without ever having been adequately resolved. The radical right is seeking to overturn the achievements of the past, while the radical left, through sporadic terrorist activity, seems intent on making it easier for the forces of reaction to become solidified.

The rapid strides in social justice made in legislation enacted during the first hundred days of the Roosevelt Administration were accomplished with overwhelming Congressional majorities. These majorities weakened in the late 1930's until at present progress has been seriously retarded. The middle ground between right and left, which I would define as the ground of rational politics, has been largely abandoned whether by politicians in the deep South or by those in the North, the East, and the far West. My colleagues to the south of Tennessee find political security in opposing any and everything even remotely connected with Civil Rights, while my colleagues north of Kentucky and west of the Rockies find similar security in voting for anything obliquely connected with Civil Rights. Though this polarization may be changing outside of the deep South, it is not clear that it is changing for the better, that is, it is not clear whether more politicians are moving towards the middle ground or are, rather, assuming a reactionary stance.

Tennessee is in mid-passage; it is a border state both geographically and politically. Here the issues are fought out in the grimmest of terms. My personal experience has been that I can make a stand and strive successfully to defend a position that is conscientiously assumed and based in reason, constitutionality, and practicality. Here there is no room for "politics as usual" (in the sordid meaning of that phrase). One's only refuge, one's only desire, must be to defend our common humanity. I have supported most of the Civil Rights bills in Congress, but I have opposed the position of those Civil Rights activists who have no appreciation of the education in sensibility which must precede and accompany any vast social reform; and I have been equally opposed to the all-out resistance attitude which characterizes the traditional Southern approach to this issue.

The question for a legislator, here as always, concerns the effective limits of law. Law cannot *per se* create higher moral standards, cannot correct deeply held prejudices, cannot engender the spirit of neighborliness. Tocqueville's observation is both timely and timeless: "Inequality is sanctioned by the manners whilst it is effaced from the laws of the country." Nevertheless, the law can remove barriers and provide opportunities. And reasonable administration of law can set a moral tone and foster an atmosphere conducive to general social progress. But the price of excessive dependence on governmental power (now for a good cause, perhaps subsequently for a bad cause) may be simply to dangerously expand the coercive powers of government, and may result in the greatest ill of all, a general restriction of liberty.

In a democracy, as I have said, the badge of citizenship is the franchise. Its intelligent exercise is the citizen's one best hope for progress. Historically, the Negro's participation in government has been erratic. During the reconstruction period he voted in relatively large numbers, though it is questionable whether during this time of military occupation his votes were entirely his own. As Bourbon control began to be reestablished in the Southern states, the Negro vote began to decline. The pattern was a ragged one and the rate of decline varied from place to place. Occasionally, Populist reformers and the neo-Bourbons vied for the Negro vote, but by the last decade of the nineteenth century both groups joined forces to disenfranchise the Negro—by intimidation, fraud, physical force, and finally by allegedly "legal" means through state laws carefully tailored to discriminatory ends.

With the passage of the Civil Rights Act of 1957, Congress moved in the voting-rights field with some degree of force and determination. I supported that bill, for it seemed to me entirely right that Congress should provide for the implementation of the rights guaranteed by the Constitution. Time proved this measure to be but a first step, for the traditions of the past were difficult to break, particularly in the deep South. It was necessary then to follow up with additional voting-rights measures in 1960, 1965, and 1970—all of which I supported.

The achievement of liberty for the Negro, although it has been slow and hesitant, is now at hand, and the effective use of the suffrage will secure it. The achievement of complete equality, however, is an entirely different matter, and it is doubtful that it will be guaranteed merely by opening hitherto barred doors. Here we are faced primarily with a task of education, of the establishment of a moral climate, of a concerned and humane tone throughout society—none of which is the subject of legislation. It can, nevertheless, be an area of some governmental activity, particularly on the part of the Executive, which must by all its actions reflect the best instincts of the national consciousness, and which therefore must do nothing that would discredit or demean the image of the underprivileged minority. Furthermore, the Executive should exemplify in a positive way its efforts to exalt the minority to a position of total equality, to elevate the minority socially, economically, intellectually, and politically, to its rightful eminence. I think it is obvious that the present Administration is fulfilling neither this negative nor this positive exemplary office.

Perhaps the most delicate issue with which I have had to deal has concerned the integration of public schools. Here we are dealing with the physical safety of small children whose very lives may sometimes be placed in jeopardy. And again there are problems brought about by the "legal" segregation, sanctioned by state and local laws and earlier Supreme Court decisions, as well as problems of attitude and of private mores. The legal difficulties seem to have been in part resolved successfully; but the revolution in moral conduct required for the acceptance of a fully integrated school system, both in the North and in the South, is not now susceptible to direct legislative action—here again the example of the Executive is essential.

While one applauds the 1954 Supreme Court decision which destroyed the pernicious "separate but equal" doctrine, one may deplore the fact that the Congress itself did little either before or immediately after that decision to eliminate segregation. Congressional legislation would have been eminently desirable, but the Eisenhower Administration was hesitant and the whole question of definition and procedure for school desegregation was left to the courts which, limited as they are, acted sometimes wisely, sometimes ineptly. Under our system of Government, the courts do not have the machinery for dealing with such problems on a nationwide basis. The irony is that the people and many of the people's representatives in Congress devoted themselves to attacking the courts rather than to advancing programs for promoting equality and justice.

When the Congress did finally decide to act in 1964, political attitudes across the nation and in Congress itself had already become radicalized and the procedure which was adopted was both ill-conceived and ill-executed. The most stringent provision of the 1964 Civil Rights Bill was one which vested unspecified, middle-rank functionaries in the Department of Health, Education, and Welfare with the power to cut off funds or to threaten to withhold funds to hospitals and to school systems—state-wide, county-wide, or individually—if any of these agencies or institutions appeared to deviate from the guidelines and regulations which the Department was to draw up and promulgate. I regarded this as an arbitrary delegation and assumption of power which would be subject to dangerous abuse. While the Senate proponents of the Bill denied that it contained this authority, or expressed voluble assurance that it would certainly never be used, the record has shown that such loosely defined powers were implicit in the Bill—and some of the same Senators who denied the effect or the intent of those provisions have since asserted and defended them.

Because of this arbitrary grant of power and because I doubted the justice and rationality of, for example, denying Federal funds to a hospital filled with sick people because the waiting rooms did not comply with undefined "guidelines," I opposed the Bill. I could not see the wisdom of cutting off funds to an entire school system, and thereby injuring all the students, because one school in a county allegedly violated a loosely constructed enforcement provision.

Now, I acknowledge that many people disagreed and will disagree with this point of view. They believe that denial of funds, whomever it may injure, is a justifiable means to a good end, and that this is the most effective way to bring about lasting change. I concede them their point of view, but I feel very deeply that I was right both with regard to the political principle involved in an undemocratic grant of power and with regard to the ethical principle of punishing many for the (real or alleged) shortcomings of a few. When some colleagues whom I respected asked me to vote for the Bill as a matter of moral principle, I acknowledged that principle was indeed involved—but involved in more ways than one—and that, moreover, Congress should enact clearly defined laws, not general principles.

The looseness and vagueness of the 1964 Civil Rights Act is also evident in that one provision would appear to *prohibit* the withholding of funds or the threat of withholding funds on failure to transport school children beyond the borders of their regular school district in order to achieve racial balance. Nevertheless the guidelines of the Department of Health, Education, and Welfare have required precisely such bussing of children, though officials of the Department say this is not done for the specific purposes forbidden by the law.

There is also a provision which states that all such rules, regulations, guidelines, interpretations, or orders "shall be uniformly applied and enforced throughout the fifty states." But the fact is that these provisions have been enforced primarily in the South, and Senator Ribicoff was entirely right when he accused other sections of the country of "monumental hypocrisy" for their failure to require equal enforcement of the Act.

Unmoved by the threat of the collapse of public education and the dangerous unravelling of the social fabric because of tensions over busing, President Nixon finally was moved by political considerations to exert the leadership he should have displayed a year earlier. On March 24th of 1970, he did finally speak out and his views, as nearly as I can determine by winnowing the thousands of words of chaff from the few grains of specific Presidential policy, appeared to run somewhat parallel to my own. But can we depend on it?

We hear much of *de facto* segregation because of housing patterns. But this need not preclude quality education if we legislate greater benefits in terms of funds and equipment for those schools which need them most. As for such housing patterns, I hope we may soon see full freedom of choice resulting from the Civil Rights Act of 1968 which I supported. It is morally wrong, and I believe unconstitutional, to place racial restrictions on the location where any American citizen may live or own property. Removal of this, it seems to me, is a much better way to achieve true integration of our society than to rely on such disruptive expedients as the improvident transportation of school children.

As I view the whole spectrum of federal action in race relations, I would break it down into three broad classifications. First, there are legal barriers to be overcome. Federal, state, and local laws and ordinances which place the Negro in a disadvantaged position can be corrected. Second, there are more positive actions which should be taken to assist the Negro to achieve social parity. I have in mind such provisions as would supply special training, additional educational facilities and funds to make up for past deficiencies, and would result in the assurance of equal employment opportunities—but I have stopped short of rigid quotas which I believe to be more likely to exacerbate rather than ameliorate relationships. Third, there are those actions through which government could seek to coerce the dominant group into accepting members of the minority group on a basis of personal equality. The federal government could, I suppose, seek to prescribe rules for social preference. But, while I would prefer all persons to be judged solely on their individual merits, there is the very real question whether an attempt to legislate personal acceptance would be counterproductive. Here, again, we are outside the realm of legislation as such and in the realm of attitude and of Presidential leadership, leadership which the Nixon Administration with its so-called "Southern Strategy" does not seem willing to supply.

In the turbulence of the present moment in history, we face an institutional breakdown. The family has become fragmented, the churches are gradually losing their interest in clear-cut social goals, and local neighborhoods are leaderless. Clearly these basic social institutions need to be strengthened and reenforced, but while we are as individual citizens pursuing this goal, we must of necessity place increasing reliance on those institutions which are functioning. Foremost among the latter, I would place the schools. It is a cliché to maintain that there has never been a time when education is more important than it is today, not only in the physical sciences in which we have excelled, but even more so in the social sciences, in that whole broad area known as "human relations." But this is a cliché precisely *because* it is so true. Our teachers and our schools must receive the highest priority, and just as I am opposed to making the schools bear the brunt of the struggle for racial equality, so am I opposed to letting them suffer in the fight against inflation. The chief resource of a nation is its young people, and to cut funds for schools as a measure for curbing inflation is to sacrifice our youth on the altar of Mammon. Even in the short-term view—much favored by the present Administration—the expansion and improvement of our educational capabilities is not inflationary since improved schooling is essential to the strength and growth of the economy. The federal government has not been allowed a full and direct role in education. Under the Constitution the maintenance of schools is a local and state responsibility—and I would not want to see this basic relationship altered. But neither would I want to see it so exaggerated that federal assistance would be severely restricted. Assistance is not synonymous with control.

Federal legislation affecting schools, as well as nearly all social legislation today in force, has had its roots in changes in our economic structure and in the accelerated pace of urbanization. We graduated from a rural to an urban society very speedily and there was, as a consequence, a considerable time-lag before the federal government could fill the needs formerly met by local and state government or by some non-governmental agencies.

We have clung nostalgically to the illusion that the family is an economic bulwark against individual hardships. In our rural society—the mentality of which still shapes much of our political thinking—the family could take in the elderly and provide for the incapacitated. But whether we approve or not, we have irreversibly moved into the era of a highly industrialized society in which the family unit is smaller and there is no traditional haven for the aged or the unfortunate. Thus we have revolutionized our concept of charity, and developed programs for a guaranteed income and medical insurance. Perhaps the most important of the social reforms of this century has been the social security system which I have been instrumental in improving, particularly with regard to Medicare.

In 1964, which was an election year for me, support of Medicare entailed considerable political risk. The greatest obstacle to the initiation of the program then was the proposal that Congress raise social security cash benefits in such a way that the payroll taxes which went into social security trust funds would reach the long-discussed "magic" level (top limit) of 10 per cent. This proposal had been put forward, in my opinion, for the express purpose of freezing out Medicare permanently. If the tax went to 10 per cent without Medicare, there would have been no funds for financing Medicare under social security then or later. And securing adoption of Medicare without tying it to existing social security programs would have been infinitely more difficult.

A system for financing through trust funds, with payroll taxes providing the revenues, was already established under social security, and following this system of financing would preclude the necessity of going through the annual appropriations process—always an uncertain and complicated route. (I believe no one would question that the Interstate Highway System would not be as nearly on schedule as it is today if financing for it were dependent on annual appropriations from general tax revenues.) I should add, however, that designating funds for specific programs to be carried out over a span of many years is definitely a poor practice in government—but politics must always lean heavily on what is possible, even though it may not be theoretically most desirable.

In 1964 it seemed clear to me that unless some member of the Senate Finance Committee took up the cause of health care for the elderly—established as a matter of right rather than through the demeaning procedure of meeting a "needs" test—Medicare might be lost forever. I took up the fight in the Committee, but lost it there and had to go to the full Senate; by this time the Administration had come forward with some support and the Senate adopted an effective program. The House did not agree, and the bill died in conference. And I bore the full brunt of responsibility.

The political campaigns of that year so clearly proved that there was public support for Medicare that the program was adopted easily in 1965. I lost a great many votes of otherwise friendly elderly constituents in 1964 because adoption of Medicare caused a delay in passage of a bill to increase social security benefits. Benefits were subsequently increased, and we had Medicare as well, but votes against me had been counted.

Though we have achieved a fairly adequate system of health benefits for the elderly, we have not yet regularized such programs for the poor. This too must be on the agenda for the future if we are to take seriously the constitutional mandate of "promoting the general welfare."

One of the great strengths of our system of government, based as it is on written texts, lies in both the spirit and the wording of these foundation documents. They were written with active verbs and affirmative phrases: "*promote* the general welfare . . . *secure* the blessings of liberty . . . *insure* domestic tranquility . . . *form* a more perfect union." These are ringing and inspiring calls to action and effort, and while not promising the millennium, they allow for, invite, suggest, and indeed, *demand* change.

It is true, the price of implementing these consitutional rights is the turmoil we presently experience in our society. It is a heavy price, but a necessary price. There can be no turning back now; our social revolution has moved forward to a point where it must complete its cycle.

6.

Ethics and Elections

BECAUSE the most vital single action of a self-governing society is the election of public officials, the election period ought to be a time of serious discussion, a time when basic political philosophies and programs are analyzed and debated—not for the sound they make but for their meaning, not for their marketability but their merit, not for their packaging but their content.

Unless the will of the people can be determined and maintained through the electoral system, there is no such thing as popular self-government. Unless the elective process itself is surrounded by ironclad safeguards, there can be no real assurance that the will of the electorate will emerge. The very phrase, "the selling of the President," points up how ineffective some of these safeguards presently are.

The principle of "one man, one vote" is no longer endangered by violations relating to the casting of ballots, the counting of ballots, or the secrecy of balloting. The danger now is much more insidious, and I shall examine it in detail shortly.

We correctly look upon voting as the exercise of one of the inalienable political rights of citizens, and through the years we have extended this right to more and more segments of the population, while concomitantly striking down laws and regulations, and correcting social prejudices which would restrict it. Though voting is a right, it is a duty as well—but an individual duty which must be decided upon personally and not coerced whether by a system of fines or by direct public pressure. As a rule, all of these various qualifications and conditions have been maintained in our electoral processes. Nevertheless, we have a long way to go in making our voting system as free, unhampered, and equitable as it should be if we are to avoid the tyranny of self-interested groups or the indifference of mass passivity.

As I have already observed, I would like to see the vote extended to 18-year-olds. The disenfranchisement of our youth may have been largely responsible for their radicalization. I would like to see the electorate vote directly for the President and Vice-President rather than through the antiquated electoral college which I do not think ought to be reformed, but abolished. I would like to see our mobile population allowed to vote in Presidential elections without fulfilling the lengthy residence requirements which currently are in force.

Perhaps the one political institution among us which has been subject to as much criticism as the electoral college is the quadrennial conventions for nominating the President and Vice-President. Though I believe the electoral college has long outlived its usefulness, I am not persuaded that we should nominate candidates for the highest offices in the land by a national primary election. Someone would have to winnow out the scores of contenders, and I know of no procedure for this which would be any less cumbersome and any more democratic than the national conventions. Though there are serious defects in the mode of selecting delegates to these conventions, and there are obvious flaws in the kind of circus atmosphere that frequently prevails, the conventions nevertheless remain an effective instrument for reaching party consensus on a given candidate. Any other procedure would have to entail a sequence of primary elections, each of which would reduce the list of possible candidates, until finally in the last primary the final decision would be reached. The cost of this, to say nothing of the confusion, would be impossible to cope with.

Moreover, the national conventions are strong forces for the preservation of the two-party structure of our politics, and I think the preservation of this structure is important. It was Disraeli who observed: "You can have no Parliamentary government, if you have no party government." Moreover, these conventions—the only occasion for political leaders and the rank and file from all the states to gather—are in the best sense of the word "educational" both for the millions who follow them on television, and for the delegates themselves. Certainly, if the Democratic Party cannot learn a great deal about itself and the state of the Union from its last convention in Chicago, then it has become more unresponsive to reality than is tolerable in any national party.

In the preceding three paragraphs I have mentioned summarily some specific aspects of the reform of our electoral process. But I have merely adverted to them briefly, because I feel that the overriding issue in safeguarding and improving our elections does not so much concern particular remedies as it concerns the whole moral climate in which political man lives. I believe one of the greatest political evils in our country is the exorbitant influence which extra-governmental financing plays in federal elections. The problem, of course, has always been with us —one of the early Tammany sachems referred to himself as simply a "marketable commodity"—but with the ever-accelerating reliance of candidates on advertising and promotion through the media the money issue has become crucial.

The Corrupt Practices Act of 1925 and the Hatch Act of 1939 continue to form the basis of existing law dealing with the financing of federal elections. Before that, in 1907, Congress passed the Tillman Act which prohibited banks and corporations from making contributions; and in 1910, for the first time, interstate political committees were required to report campaign expenditures and contributions, and to identify the source of all donations over $100. Though these laws have been amended from time to time, they are today completely inadequate. And, unfortunately, there is no widespread public concern over the threat to popular government which arises from the uncontrolled influence of the moneyed interests in our elections.

Although not many people would sell their vote, they may in effect be robbed of it by the manipulation of the mass media. Few people are entirely immune to the flood of propaganda, advertising, and promotion techniques which are at the disposition of any well-financed candidate. This merchandising of candidates like detergents and cosmetics undermines the entire electoral process since in effect it restricts the exercise of free choice among great numbers of people—particularly the poorly educated who are still susceptible to the increasingly subtle and refined blandishments of the media.

In order to determine the over-all extent of the problem,

and more particularly to learn the source of political contributions, to see how well they were recorded and where they were spent, the Senate in 1956 authorized the Subcommittee on Privileges and Elections to investigate the Presidential election of that year. I was chairman of this group, and the resulting report was the largest and most heavily documented study ever reported to the Senate on *any* subject; it is still the only comprehensive assessment of the matter. Though the closely printed volume was the size of a major city telephone directory, interest in its findings was so great that the demand for copies could not be met. Nevertheless, it was clear to me and my colleagues, Senator Mike Mansfield and Senator Carl T. Curtis, that this report was not exhaustive. But since it is the only report of its kind, some of its findings deserve to be detailed here.

We were able to identify the source of over $33 million spent in the 1956 elections by the major political parties and political action groups. But the total amount was of course much higher than this figure. The breakdown of expenditures was as follows:

Republican	$20,685,387
Democratic	10,977,790
Labor	941,271
Miscellaneous	581,277

The largest single expenditure in this election was for television and radio time. During the period from September 1 to November 6, the two major parties spent a total of $9,501,000 on television and radio for all political offices. Again, this figure represents only what we were able to document; there is no doubt that more money in fact was spent on the media. The actual breakdown of contributions disclosed little that was new to the committee: Republican contributions came primarily from wealthy individuals and people associated with the large corporations, while labor's contributions went primarily to Democratic committees and candidates.

What was more significant, however, was the geographical distribution of political contributions. New York was the major source of individual contributions to both parties—as one would have expected; but one might not have expected it to be so overwhelmingly, so preponderantly Republican. Contributions of $500 or more made by individuals in New York to Republican candidates and committees totaled $2,382,047—almost equal to the total aggregate of $2,820,655 of such contributions made to Democratic candidates in *all* the states (including New York).

Without imputing wrongdoing to individuals or to the recipient committees, the report noted that a fuller recording of contributions . . .

> "is for all practical purposes meaningless because it is applicable only to political committees as defined in the law and there is no prohibition upon the making of multiple contributions in the maximum amount to any number of such committees. Furthermore, the law is not applicable at all to a contribution made to an organization which does not operate in two or more states and is not a branch of a political party. Thus it would be possible for one member of a wealthy family to make a single contribution of $100,000 to the Republican (or Democratic) Finance Committee of New York without any apparent violation of the Corrupt Practices Act."

Also, we pointed out that notwithstanding the apparent prohibition in that Act against the making of expenditures by corporations and labor unions, there appeared to be an uncontrollably broad area of permissible activity in the light of the loose judicial interpretation placed upon the term "expenditure." The Subcommittee therefore advocated that there should be a "specialized and intensive study of the activities of both labor unions and corporations in federal elections." We observed that existing statutory provisions were inadequate, and advocated the preparation of "amendatory legislation" which would require "careful assimilation of additional factual information and thorough analysis of the Constitutional issues involved."

The need for remedial legislation is even more imperative today. Very little has changed, and where changes have occurred they have often been more disadvantageous than was the status quo ante. Thus the amount spent has continued to increase drastically, and the Congress has had to contend with three spectacular cases of ethics, all focusing in one way or another on financial responsibility: the case of Thomas Dodd, of Adam Powell, and of Bobby Baker.

Public confidence in government, and in the integrity of the people's representatives who constitute that government, is the bedrock upon which the foundation of our entire social order rests. Government is only as secure as the public's faith in it. Moreover, representative government cannot be *truly* representative unless the electorate has an opportunity to choose among candidates on the basis of their qualifications without improper or undue influences which impede freedom of choice. There is something profoundly wrong about a system in which the election of a senator costs one million dollars—the conservative estimate of what is needed to unseat an incumbent in the average industrial state. Such a large amount of money is obviously not expended for the instruction of the electorate or with a view to airing fundamental political differences: it is spent with a view to trying to brainwash the citizenry.

Moreover, that portion of the public which doesn't succumb to such procedures is probably totally disillusioned about the integrity of our political leaders. Few people imagine that such expensive campaigns are financed by the small contributions of public-spirited citizens; they know that even if large contributions do come "without strings attached," it is obvious that the wealthy contributor stands on an entirely different footing from other constituents when matters of concern to both come up for decision by elected officials. Even the absence of self-serving motives on the part of the giver, the receiver, or both cannot entirely erase the influence of large campaign contributions because the candidate who refuses to accept this kind of money is placed at an immense disadvantage. The disillusioned public knows that money can *buy* an election without any of our archaic election laws having been directly violated, and without the victorious candidate "buying" a single vote.

It was because of the almost unendurable expenses involved in campaigning that former Senator Paul Douglas referred to them as "one of the most corrupting influences in public life." For an example, an advertising concern, acting entirely upon its own initiative, submitted a proposed budget for my 1970 campaign—$795,000 for advertising alone. There were a number of grounds for not accepting such a proposal, including the obvious practical reason. Moreover, assuming that both candidates do have such funds at their disposal for campaigning in a state such as my own, will the public good be served in any way commensurate with the immensity of these amounts of money? Since the public has a relatively low saturation point for public-affairs broadcasts of any kind, most of this money would not go into discussion of the issues, but into various manipulative techniques and promotional devices. Such gimmickry is generally abhorrent to the candidate, is insulting to the electorate, and is totally detrimental to the political health of the nation.

Moreover, in addition to direct campaign costs, there are the financial requirements of election procedures on the district level. Though ideally the implementation of such procedures should be entirely a matter for citizen participation and party initiative, the actual task of registration and "getting out the vote" is generally relegated or assumed by special-interest groups and labor organizations. Expenses related to these two functions are probably the largest single political cost at the local level. Volunteer labor suffices in some areas, and this of course is preferable, but generally the local leaders of each party pay considerable sums to hire workers, ballot watchers, chauffeurs, etc.

Of course, even if it could be assumed with any degree of certainty that those contributing to the financing of political campaigns would expect and receive nothing more than good government, and could it be established that no Member of Congress or other elected official would be influenced to vote or otherwise favor those contributing to his campaign directly, there would still be ample cause foı concern over the high cost of political campaigns and the manner of raising money for their conduct. In 1968, reported expenditures for campaigns for Federal offices amounted to about $70 million, and responsible estimates of the total cost of electing the President in that year have run as high as $100 million. Such tremendous expenditures clearly illustrate the necessity for access to big money. True democratic processes can hardly long survive under such circumstances. A new power elite is emerging—the power of money has replaced hereditary power.

And there is an even further danger now. With the looseness with which campaign contributions are handled, with no rigid accounting required, with the laws structured in such a way as to encourage a multiplicity of committees to receive contributions, there is a great temptation for the candidate and his closest supporters to siphon off a sizable portion of campaign contributions and pocket them for their own personal use. This is venality at its worst, and its psychological ramifications are not distinguished from bribery.

Almost everyone in political life agrees that some reform is needed. With such unanimity, it is remarkable that the laws have not been changed—but given the nature of elective office, it is also somewhat understandable. In a non-election year, it is difficult to arouse public concern, whereas in an election year perfectly valid arguments can be mustered against appearing to advocate changing the rules in, as it were, the middle of the game. Modifications in the law must be approved by officials who have been chosen under the present system. It is not entirely an unreasonable fear on their part that any change might adversely affect their own campaign for reelection. People instinctively shy away from relying on untested procedures when they have been personally well-served by the tested ones. Nevertheless, I see no other way for eliminating the stench of private money from the elective process than public financing for campaigns to federal offices.

This is not a novel suggestion. In fact, a half century after Theodore Roosevelt first advocated some governmental subsidy, a bill was passed that would have provided public funds for the Presidential campaign. I led a successful fight the following year to have it rendered inoperable before it took effect. Nor in this do I think I was in any way inconsistent, since I thought the proposal by Senator Russell Long was extremely simplistic. His plan provided that each taxpayer on his income tax return would have the opportunity of indicating that one dollar of his tax payment would be set aside for a fund to be divided equally between the Republican and Democratic candidates for President.

Being concerned, as I have indicated in the preceding chapters, about the establishment of dangerous legal precedents, I feared that if this scheme were to gain popular currency, public pressures would be exerted, and taxpayers might be clamoring for additional provisions allowing them to personally designate tax moneys for this or that specific purpose. Both because the allocation of tax revenues is a constitutional function of the Congress, and because of the fiscal irresponsibility that might ultimately result from any such system as the Long bill could initiate, I was opposed to it.

However, the mechanics of the proposal was by far a secondary consideration. Under Senator Long's bill, the candidates of the two major parties would receive millions of dollars in federal money without any effective control over its expenditure, and without any restrictions *whatever* to curtail already existing practices for soliciting private funds. Under this plan, the major parties could continue to raise as much money as possible from whatever sources, with public funds simply functioning as supplementary income. With incredible naïveté, it was argued that if public funds were made available to Presidential candidates, there would be no need to raise money from questionable sources, and, as a consequence, all the political evils associated with election financing would utterly evaporate. Needless to say, this is the politics of utopia; it is not the politics of America. It is generally by their own affidavit that candidates or public officials arguing along these lines prove their own selflessness. An antidote to original sin is presumably just around the corner.

My own proposals for subsidizing federal elections are contained in a bill which the Senate Finance Committee approved in 1968, and which I reintroduced with further clarifications in 1970. A major feature of the proposal is that it would require the candidate himself to choose between public and private financing. Appropriate funds would be made available to the candidate in an amount pre-determined as sufficient to defray reasonable campaign expenditures—but once he accepted public money, he would be required to forego entirely all private contributions. As to the latter, the bill would also regulate more closely both the raising and the spending of such money.

After two decades of frustration, it would be unrealistic to be overly sanguine about the passage of such a bill, even though it does contain some unique features designed, quite frankly, to make it more palatable to my colleagues. Thus, it applies only to Presidential and Senatorial campaigns, but not to those for the House of Representatives. If the bill can be passed in the Senate, the House would be free to advance its own proposals for its own members. Another feature is that the bill would not go into effect until 1975. With an effective date more than four years hence, the provisions of such a law would not affect the re-election of any member now serving in the Senate. No Senator voting for the bill could therefore be viewed as trying to gain access to public funds for his own re-election campaign.

The third major feature of my election reform proposal seeks to remove the cost of radio and television time from the candidates' budgets by directing the Federal Communications Commission—after appropriate notice and hearings—to promulgate regulations requiring licensees of the commercial stations to make available, without charge and on a fair and equitable basis, broadcast time to qualified candidates for federal office. A survey of the three major networks shows expenditures in the 1968 campaign of $4.2 million by Republicans, and $2.5 million by Democrats and $681,000 by George Wallace—on the three major networks *alone*. Prices increased 25 per cent between the 1964 and the 1968 elections, and raised the cost of a 60 second nationally televised announcement to $65,000. Such costs are unendurable, and must be obviated either by some such proposal as that which I have incorporated into my bill, or that of the Twentieth-Century Fund whereby the federal government would purchase nationwide television and radio time to be apportioned among the various candidates. Though the cost of the latter might be prohibitive, the suggestion certainly represents one step in the right direction.

And even the bill which I have introduced is only a first step. I would hope that eventually all stages of the federally elective process, primaries and conventions as well as the general election, will be publicly financed under regulations which will limit spending to amounts reasonably necessary to inform the electorate, and with rigid controls enforced on the expenditure of all funds.

Until we have direct federal subsidy of election campaigns, we must restrict the size of contributions and the number of individual contributions allowed; and even more important, we must broaden the base to include greater numbers of our citizens. One instrument for effecting this kind of participatory democracy would be to offer a partial tax-exemption or tax-incentive plan. Apart from the obvious benefits, this might also induce people to place a higher value on the votes they cast. I emphasize "value," and by this I do not mean "price tag." Due to our equation of money with elections, even among the well intentioned these two terms are regarded as synonymous—as was illustrated by one of the campaigns sponsored by the American Heritage Foundation to increase the flow of private contributions to candidates to public office. Slogans like, "I think my dollar as important as my vote," "You have got to pay your way to have your say," etc., reflected not only bad pedagogy, but bad political theory as well. No dollar is as important to any American as is his franchise, and all men and women who are qualified to vote have an equal say at the ballot box whether they contribute a large or a small sum. Of course, the slogans were composed by the agency people and account executives who have already done so much to identify our elective system with the buying and selling of commodities.

But germane to all these public reforms are the reforms needed in the Congress itself. The reformer must reform himself at the same time he seeks to reform others. This matter of personal ethics touches upon some of the most delicate issues, and some of the most scandalous blots our chief lawmaking body has experienced. I have already alluded to such confidence-eroding cases as those of Senator Dodd and Congressman Powell. These represent perhaps the more extreme instances and underline only more blatantly the need for closer regulation of private Congressional finances.

For instance, an individual candidate or incumbent must now use his own judgment in determining what are "campaign" expenditures and what are personal expenditures. Many incumbents maintain a "campaign" fund for use at all times since—certainly in the House of Representatives—they may be regarded as constantly campaigning. It may be recalled that President Nixon, when a Senator and campaigning for the Vice-Presidency, had his integrity seriously impugned by critics who questioned his use of a "fund" furnished to him by loyal followers.

The Nixon incident exemplifies both the complexity of the question, and the need for stricter controls and clearer guidelines. But while the Congress has been insistent, and rightly so, on the establishment and acceptance of such guidelines for the courts and the Executive branch, it has failed almost completely to police itself, and it is apparently unwilling to make a serious effort to do so. Moreover, since Congress is an "irresponsible" body—that is, a body not directly answerable to either of the other two branches—there is simply no agency to police it. The irony of this is pointed up by the fact that Congress has enacted seven general conflict-of-interest laws, as well as the bribery statutes. And when a nominee either for the Executive or the Judicial branch comes before the Senate for confirmation, his personal finances, business connections, and social relationships are displayed to full public view. As is only right and proper, the Senate has been particularly concerned with nominees who have large holdings in corporations doing substantial business with the government, particularly when the company concerned deals directly with the department or agency to which the nominee may be appointed.

But when a Congressman or Senator is elected by popular vote his possible conflict of interest is not generally further reviewed. Indeed, only two of the seven general conflict-of-interest laws are even applicable to members of Congress. The bribery laws do, of course, apply; but we are dealing with problems which only very rarely could be technically defined as bribery. This makes the matter all the more vague and elusive. Certainly, no Congressman would employ such a direct and detectable approach as that of Daniel Webster when he asked Nicholas Biddle for the "usual retainers" for representing the interests of Biddle's banks from his prestigious seat in the Senate.

But what of lawyers who come to the Congress and retain membership in law firms from which they derive substantial sums of money during their elected tenure? Much, of course, would depend upon the identity of clients, the services rendered, the nature of the remuneration—all precisely the very areas in which disclosure is not required. A Senator must report a lecture fee, say, at a university, or a fee for writing an article; but somehow the Senate has concluded that a legal fee or income from a law firm need not be reported. The rationale usually supplied for this contradictory situation is that such a report would disclose the lawyer-client relationship—exactly what *should be* disclosed. It is common knowledge that just a few years ago the chairman of a Senate committee having considerable responsibility for legislation directly affecting railroads was an active partner in a law firm which represented *several* railroads. In this case, however, the matter became an issue in his campaign for re-election, and he was involuntarily retired by the people of his state.

According to reports filed in 1969 with the House Committee on Standards of Official Conduct—generally known as the House Ethics Committee—92 Congressmen were directors, officers, board chairmen, or stockholders in banks, savings and loan associations, bank holding companies, or other financial institutions. Thirteen of these Congressmen were members of the House Banking and Currency Committee. Of course, not all of these 13 consistently voted against needed reforms; indeed, a few were widely recognized champions of the public interest. But such is rarely the case.

We might, for instance, examine a measure approved in 1970 which would allow states to tax national banks just as they now tax state-chartered banks with which they compete. Although the proposal seemed obviously a fair one, during debate on this bill in the House a determined effort was made to secure adoption of an amendment which would have prevented state taxation of certain important profits of the larger national banks, and thus preserve for them a preferential position. Notwithstanding the fact that this was patently contrary to the many "state's rights" speeches of some of its advocates, it was ardently defended by some members of the Banking and Currency Committee who, along with their families, had large banking holdings.

Let us consider the considerably more delicate problem which arises from the making of Committee assignments because of constituent interest. A Congressman or a Senator with a primarily agricultural constituency wishes to be assigned to the Agricultural Committee. A Senator from an oil-producing state not only wishes to serve on the Finance Committee, but is very cautious about who else goes on such a committee. The congressman with major military installations in his district insists upon being on the Armed Services Committee or the Appropriations Committee. Now, none of this is without its merits—as well as its abuses. It is largely representative of the whole Madisonian principle of democracy in which various regional or particularized interests counterbalance one another. There is a problem, however, when constituent interest and self-interest converge.

For instance, Senator Russell Long, chairman of the Senate Finance Committee, stated in 1970 on a nationally televised program that the oil industry is very important to his state since it "accounts for about 40 per cent of all the jobs in Louisiana." And he added, "now most of my income comes from oil." Senator Long can thus unabashedly say that in representing the oil interests he is representing his constituents' interests and, incidentally, his own. One may regard this as entirely reasonable, but it becomes a very pointed issue when one is in a powerful position to affect tax legislation that may be in both his constituents' interest and his own—but contrary to the national public interest.

The Senate was very insistent that Charles E. Wilson divest himself of $2.5 million worth of stock in General Motors before he be named Secretary of Defense, because General Motors was one of the largest prime contractors with the government particularly through the Defense Department. Without the divestment of his stock, what was good for General Motors would obviously have been good for Mr. Wilson, and as the telling dictum went, "What's good for General Motors is good for the country." Presumptively, what is good for a state may be good for its Senator, *and* also good for the country. Undeniably there is some value, particularly from the standpoint of knowledge and understanding of a particular industry, trade, or commodity in having an elected representative familiar with one or another of these areas; but the value diminishes in direct proportion to his *financial involvement* in the industry, trade, or commodity in question.

All of which is merely to say that Congressmen and Senators occupy a very privileged and honored position, and therefore should abide by ethical standards which are more rigid, more elevated than those prevailing in other professions. Is not this implicit in the term "public servant"?

There are rewards other than monetary for service in the Congress: one's voice is magnified, one's strength multiplied, one's reach lengthened, one's power of accomplishment augmented, and one's views respected. Ability to achieve such a position, then, should depend neither upon the amount of money which one may possess, nor the amount of money which one can successfully solicit from special interest groups. The position itself is not, and I doubt if it should be, richly remunerative. It is sometimes said that only by increasing Congressional salaries will talented people be induced to seek such public offices. The opposite, of course, is true: the loftiness of the position itself is its own first reward, and it should not be made a prize for venal careerists. In passing, I would note that to me it is utterly ridiculous to assert that Senators and Congressmen cannot live on $30,000 or $40,000 a year; 99 per cent of the people in the country live on less. Admittedly, living expenses of Senators are higher than those of most comparable professional people, particularly for those members who maintain a home both in Washington and in their state. However, I do agree that elected representatives of the people should not have to pay from their own salary for travel on official business as they now do. But the opposite side of this coin, as I emphasized earlier, is that under no conditions should personal expenditures be drawn from political finances.

I conclude with a rather Lincolnesque anecdote, a homely story, but one not without its point. A college classmate, now a successful and very wealthy businessman, was amazed when, after telling him of the multiple duties, travels, and responsibilities of a Senator, I observed in response to his question that the salary was $42,500 a year. He expressed astonishment and suggested that for all the work involved one could become a millionaire. "But don't you think the privilege of serving in the United States Senate is worth a million?" I countered. "Yes," he said, "when do I take my seat?"

Well, some seats, I am sorry to relate, will likely be *had* in elections in 1970 for less than a million, and several are likely to be *had* for more. Yet we are supposed to be a government of, by, and for the people. It is time we began to live up to that definition.

7.

Order and Society

GOVERNMENT without the power of coercion is anarchy—no government at all. But the type, the degree, and the spirit of coercion and the manner of its implementation constitute the measure of a democratic or an autocratic society.

All law is an infringement upon individual freedom. In a sense, every traffic light, an elementary example of regulatory law, impedes progress when it flashes red. Yet traffic lights, like laws generally, mean not less but more freedom for all. In a comparable, though more sophisticated sense, this same relationship between freedom and coercion prevails in the whole area of law and rights, of duty and response, ranging from the private citizen to industry, to labor unions, and to international affairs.

The rule of law must be enthroned both in the social order and in the minds of the citizens. However, we are concerned here not simply with that kind of law which the strong can always impose on the weak, but rather with a legal order which represents the true distillation of our best instincts and of our most finely cultivated responsibilities. Thus, while order is absolutely necessary to any organization, it is not the order attained by sacrifice of freedom of speech, nor the ordered conformity which is purchased at the price of the right to dissent. In this sense, true democratic order is not something which can be arbitrarily imposed upon a free society or upon its free members. It must develop from within the society and be acceptable to all its members. And it can so develop only when there is the exercise of justice on the part of legal institutions, and a recognized need for discipline on the part of the individual citizen.

Both institutional justice and personal self-discipline are being called in question during this, one of the most turbulent periods of our national life. Ours is a time marked by upheaval and violence, by civil disobedience, organized crime, tax avoidance, wrongful conversion of corporate assets, special privilege, and challenged credibility. Social upheavals, the reassessment of past practices, the questioning of values, have occurred at intervals in our history, as they must of necessity occur in all progressive societies which test and challenge the status quo. Such inevitable frictions lie just beneath the surface at all times, fermenting, simmering, awaiting some extraordinary event or set of circumstances to explode through the crust of established custom and tradition. What is essential is that the power released by this explosive force be guided into creative rather than into destructive channels.

Our newspapers, television, and radio regularly call our attention to crime, disorder, and violent dissent. Unfortunately, they are most apt to feature street and campus disorders rather than white-collar crime or the operations of the Mafia and other organized groups which are rending in a much more profound way the fabric of our social order.

While there is no question whatever that the concept of "law and order" represents one of our noblest ideals, there is serious question as to whether the invocation of this concept as a kind of shibboleth to suppress certain minority groups, or certain dissenting activities, is really consonant with the best of our traditions. "Law and order" ought not to be made a divisive slogan applicable only to certain segments of our society—and but rarely applied to the genuinely disruptive segment of society: organized criminals. There is a real danger that in reducing this noble principle of obedience to law to a highly selective repressive measure, the real violators of "law and order" will be either unconsciously overlooked or intentionally bypassed. Obedience to law is an obligation of all and must be equally required of each. It is not a selective injunction, but a universal dictate.

Public preoccupation with violation of the law by individuals, while ignoring it on the corporate and institutional level, is fostered by its dramatic news-making character, particularly as depicted by television and photographic journalism. Certainly street disorders and other public crimes appear to be much more visibly significant than do the subtle, though more deadly and pervasive, activities of the Mafia and other criminal syndicates. But in all fairness it must be recognized that such concentration on the visible and the sensational is a liability of the media which many enlightened newsmen themselves recognize. Still this kind of narrow focus must be guarded against lest we equate civil disobedience and the violence of small groups with widespread white-collar crime and the insidious operations of the Mafia. The former may be a thorn in the side, the latter is a dagger at the heart.

But we are still not at the crux of the issue. There are historical antecedents to much of the criminal activity which is occurring today. We witnessed highly organized crime during prohibition days; and we have, many times in the past, seen various city administrations, and even state governments, fall under the influence of political gangs—sometimes composed of the recognized criminal type, sometimes of the corporate and industrial type, and, more often, of the venal politician type. We have experienced lawlessness on the frontier, Indian wars, even a national civil war.

The real crux of the matter does not pertain to controlling organized crime, or individual or group violence, though this is necessary. The real crux—the "crunch"—is in creating a solidly established, firmly grounded society which supports its government because it recognizes it as the legitimate agency for protecting and advancing the common good. Police power and coercion are essential, essential as a tourniquet to a bleeding man; but no one would want to live out his days (which would surely be brief) encumbered by a tourniquet. Police power and coercion are no substitute for surgery or the healing power of the body politic itself.

Today such healthy forces, as well as the will to heal our common social ailments, seem to be impaired. Our danger today lies not so much in violence, nor in the correctives to violence, as in the inner deterioration of our society. A deteriorated society may be shredded by the least violent outburst. It is not the tourniquet, the coercive remedy, that we must concentrate on, but rather on the causes, on the susceptibility of the entire body politic to feverish illness and even paranoiac derangement. We must first look at these causes in their institutional embodiment, and then at them in their individual manifestations, since the institution is merely the lengthened shadow of the individual.

In all social theory the family, regardless of its particular cultural components, has been both the symbol and the reality of social order and stability. And both as symbol and reality the family has been subject to the same attrition as most other elements of our culture. Prior to World War II the divorce rate was relatively low, amounting in 1940 to 2.0 per thousand of population. But in 1945 in the aftermath of a long and exhausting war, the divorce rate jumped to twice its 1940 level. At present, there is a divorce for every four marriages performed in this country. Of course, I do not question the justification of divorce, I only cite the incidence of family break-up as symptomatic of the strain on all our traditional institutions.

With the gradual disintegration of the large family group, increased mobility has also contributed to social stress and disorder. After World War II there was an extensive movement, which still continues into our larger northern cities, of black and white people, who were ill-prepared for the crowded conditions of urban living. And the congestion itself, particularly the shortage of adequate housing—intensified by the government tight-money, high-interest policy to fight inflation—created further problems. Concurrent with this ingress, the more affluent city-dwellers moved to the suburbs and thus left their former neighborhoods without effective local leadership. Such moving back and forth by large groups of people has not only resulted in a decrease in the tax base, but even more important, it has created greater tension in the changing neighborhoods—that is, in most of the central areas of our major cities.

Our people, particularly our young, are caught up in the wave of rising expectations we have commonly thought of in connection with more backward countries. We often dismiss disorders in those African, Asian, and Latin American nations with the glib remark that their people, having had a glimpse of what a better life could be like, are filled with despair at the impossibility of reaching such a future. What many in our country do not seem to understand, or do not want to admit, is that the same revolution of rising expectations, unmet and with no apparent hope of fulfillment, leads to disorder and unrest in our own streets.

It is almost impossible for the typical middle-class American to imagine what thoughts go through the mind of a fourteen-year-old ghetto boy as he watches on television youngsters from more economically secure homes playing tennis at a country club, riding sleek horses along woodland trails, cruising around a cool lake on water skis behind a high-powered motor boat. He knows these things are available. He knows, too, they are not available to him. It is obvious what he is going to believe when he is told in school and elsewhere that we are a nation of equality, that we do not believe in special privilege but in equal rights for all, etc. This splendid rhetoric will be smothered by the obvious realities. We have had too many slogans, catch-phrases, empty promises—whether consoling or insulting, whether "black capitalism" or "benign neglect." Such effete rhetoric untuned to reality can only result in confusion, in loss of faith and stability, and possibly in disorder and violence.

On the other side of the rhetorical coin, we have until lately been fortunately able to avoid the imagery of oppression and suppression so common in the literature of European social historians of whatever doctrinaire hue. Though class-war rhetoricians are emerging in a number of places in our country, I do not believe that the generality of Americans visualize themselves as being divided into exploiters and exploited, with the police apparatus primarily engaged in supporting the former against the latter. If we continue to regard equality as an attainable goal of every American in the future, we must substitute action for rhetoric and effect major social reforms.

While I think it is absurd to speak in terms of our society being polarized between the exploiters and the exploited, there is some basis for fearing that we may become a society divided between the calloused and the vulnerable. The affluent among us seem to have little understanding of the tensions under which lower paid, non-unionized, unskilled, hourly workers live. It can only be the most calloused among us who would classify such poor people as congenitally lazy, unwilling to work, and only too happy to ride the relief rolls. Perhaps some of the poor have adjusted to a welfare way of life; if so, I wonder whether their surface peace and apparent accommodation doesn't masquerade a bitter resentment towards a society which gives them no hope of improvement. Certainly one would have to be calloused to ignore the fact that some 25 million people in this country are still in the grip of poverty; two-thirds of them are white, and one-half of them live in the South. One can get some index of these deplorable conditions by considering that fully one-third of our poor people live in families whose head works *full time*.

Periods of inflation such as we are now enduring only intensify the insecurity of the poor. It is their jobs in marginal and unskilled fields that are the first to be wiped out. Since they are forced to buy on credit, they are necessarily the one segment of the population which suffers most from increased interest rates. And when they see, as they do daily, that they must pay a sales tax on each hard-earned dollar spent for food and clothing, precisely the same sales tax that the wealthy pay, they cannot but conclude that the political and economic dice are loaded against them.

As I earlier noted, Congress yielded to the insistence

of the Nixon Administration and cut the top tax rate for earned income (for instance, salaries and bonuses for corporate executives) to 50 per cent. Who could be so callous as not to recognize the injustice of a tax of 14 per cent on any part of a family income of $5000 per year when the $500,000 per year salaried executive can retain from his salary more than $250,000—a quarter of a million dollars annually? Our tax system truly takes from the poor what they have not, while leaving relatively untouched the abundance of the rich.

In the face of what must appear to them as almost systematic injustice, who can be surprised that it is the poor and underprivileged who more and more are tempted to resort to violence? Only three alternatives are in fact presented them: supine passivity, revolutionary overthrow of the existing order, or direct ameliorative political action. The first is unthinkable because inhuman; the second is foolish because counter-productive. It is the third way of struggle against injustice that must engage the vulnerable poor and the "uncalloused majority."

The storms of social and technological change are moving through our nation. The uncalloused majority, recognizing the inequities and injustices about them, welcome these winds of change as the harbinger of a second spring for America. It will require a revolution—not the military revolution which ushered in the first spring, but a revolution of human sensibility, a revolution of good will which seeks to bind up the wounds of the vulnerable poor, the dispossessed, and the disenchanted. We must harness these new forces of change blowing across the land. It is pointlessly idle to long for a less-troubled past that really never was or for a return to conditions that really never should have been. It is by our response to the forces of change that we shall be measured, both by our own consciences and by history.

The great danger is that the challenge of the future may appear so overwhelming to the weak-hearted among us, to those who have little faith in the people but only in elitist managers and manipulators, that they will believe no consciously meaningful response is possible. Existing institutions, delicately balanced political and social forces, the equations of economic need, however frequently defective, will be simply destroyed. A new beginning may be made from these ashes of the past, but only after a long period of suffering in which the condition of the weak and impoverished will reach even greater depths of degradation. We simply have no alternative but to move out from where we are, to take a longer step in the endless march of civilization. No doubt as we move into this future, some customs and certain social mores will be transcended. Some institutions will fail and be replaced by others more responsive to new needs. But we must begin where we are. There is no escaping the present if we want to start towards the future. It is to this properly political office that I now turn.

In a society which has been obsessed, for good or bad reasons, with the concept of "law and order," one immediate and essential demand is the improvement of our judicial system. The administration of justice must be more systematic; dockets must be cleared to give to the accused a speedy and just trial. Law courts must not be turned into forums of propaganda or into Star Chambers. I think the judiciary has been remiss in energetically performing its proper function. To take a specific example in the federal system, the district courts are not now experiencing any sharp increase in new cases. Nevertheless, the volume of cases continues to grow because of lethargic judicial procedures. At the end of September, 1969, more than 110,000 cases were pending before district courts, the highest figure in history.

The axiom that justice delayed is justice denied remains valid, and the results of delays in bringing cases to trial are now more far-reaching than ever in creating discontent and doubts about the proper administration of justice on all levels. Unfortunately, the lazy, incompetent, incapacitated judge cannot be dismissed under present law. The only remedy is impeachment, for which traditionally the grounds have had to be much more serious than merely age or incapacity. One witness before the Senate Judiciary Committee recently described the situation: "A federal judge may be afflicted with a helpless insanity or senility; he may be deaf and blind; he may be a hopeless alcoholic; he may be convicted of arson, murder and burglary; he may render asunder the canons of judicial ethics—he may be guilty of taking bribes and selling his justice. Common sense dictates that such a judge should not continue to occupy judicial office." Though there is considerable hyperbole in all this, it serves to indicate the seriousness of the problem and the absurdity of any solution by way of Congressional impeachment. The matter cannot be resolved by taking that road, unless we are willing to impair the independence of the judiciary—an action that might create greater problems than the ones we now face.

Nor would the appointment of additional judges do anything more than temporarily alleviate the situation. We would still have the old and incompetent on the bench. But it would in no way be an encroachment upon the principle of separation of powers for the Congress to enforce retirement at a certain age. I have therefore wholeheartedly supported all efforts at retiring judges when they reach 70 years. Such judges would still be available for whatever duties they might wish to perform, and in fact many who have voluntarily retired do continue to render valuable service. If we could make way for young, vigorous men on the bench there is no doubt that the quality of court proceedings would be improved. One does not need to go beyond the federal judiciary to realize this fact: all the country suffered through the shocking disorder and injudiciousness of the Chicago trial during the winter of 1969–70.

The judiciary must not only be fair, but as cleanly above suspicion as is humanly and institutionally possible. If the public does not have complete confidence in the impartiality and honesty of the courts, our system of justice will soon be in jeopardy; and if the public sense of justice is in question, then our whole democratic order is in question. I think it is obvious that the shock to public confidence in our courts, particularly our highest court, from the Fortas-Haynsworth-Carswell imbroglio is immeasurable. Fortunately (thanks largely to the U.S. Senate), even this had a happy ending from which we can take heart—the unanimous confirmation of Justice Harry Blackmun, a legal scholar with demonstrated judicial attributes.

Traditionally the definition of crime and the enforcement of criminal laws of the United States has been primarily a prerogative and duty of the states, and of various local governmental units. This is as it ought to be, and precisely where the primary responsibility should rest. The federal government should provide financial aid and technical assistance, and otherwise cooperate and strengthen law enforcement arms of the states. But more and more of late, the feeling seems to have spread across the land and into the highest levels of the executive branch that the federal government must assume nearly total responsibility for order in our society—that Washington must put all to right. The fact is Washington cannot; and the central government should neither be asked nor allowed to try to solve all of society's ills, least of all petty crime in the streets or sporadic and unorganized violent outbursts.

A recently released study by the Advisory Commission on Intergovernmental Relations, a 26-member bi-partisan group, indicates that public opinion is now moving away from the belief that the federal government is a better agent for crime control than are state and local governments. If this trend has been correctly assessed by the panel, there is hope for a less unbalanced federalism than we have experienced in the recent past. State and local governments have essential functions to perform. Indeed, democracy fails totally unless it works at the community level. And nowhere is this more obviously true than in the maintenance of order. Our cherished system of checks and balances includes the maintenance of state power to counterbalance federal power; and in like manner the local governments, and even the local communities, act as controlling influences on the larger correlative governmental bodies.

Paradoxically, the most strident voices clamoring for massive "law and order" crusades insist that they should be led by the federal government. Yet these same voices, in the next breath, will deplore the disappearance of "states' rights." For such politicians, inconsistency is going to prove to be only a temporary refuge from the virtues of logic. Though I have advocated an enlarged federal role in many fields—education, economic management, social justice—I do not want to see enforcement of local order and local ordinances centered in Washington. If we are to avoid even the faintest hint of an incipient totalitarianism, the police power should be diffused through all the communities of the nation.

Of course it would be absurd to suggest that there is not an important role for the federal government in crime prevention and in maintaining order. Congress itself recognized the pluralistic nature of law enforcement in its "Omnibus Crime Control and Safe Streets Act of 1968":

> "Congress finds that the high incidence of crime in the United States threatens the peace, the security, and general welfare of the nation and its citizens. To prevent crime and to insure the greater safety of the people, law enforcement efforts must be better coordinated, intensified, and made more effective at all levels of government. Congress finds further that crime is essentially a local problem that must be dealt with by state and local governments if it is to be controlled effectively."

Problems which are truly national in scope, such as organized crime and illicit drug traffic have in fact received the urgent attention of the Congress, which in 1970 passed the "Organized Crime Control Act" and "The Controlled Dangerous Substances Act." Drug traffic in particular must be brought under control, for the drastic increase in narcotics addiction in recent years appears to be directly related to the alarming increase in crime, particularly in larceny, robbery, and burglary.

All of this represents what the federal government *can* do. Precisely what it cannot do, or must not do, is, first, create the framework for what might ultimately be a national system of policing and surveillance; and second—as I have observed previously in this book with regard to tariffs and to racial integration—bring to bear the immense powers of the federal government for the implementation of *ad hoc* solutions—solutions which, however effective in the immediate present, are in the long run an affront to the very principles that they are alleged to preserve.

In the first instance I have reference to the army's data

bank on dissenting citizens—a collection of facts, and possibly fictions, which presumably embraces everyone from the most violent Minuteman or Weatherman to the most elderly and genteel signatories of peace petitions. In the second instance, one may be more precise about what is being derided, because unlike the situation of the data bank, no effort whatever has been made to conceal it: in fact it has been trumpeted from the housetops as one of the glories of the present Administration. I refer to the Attorney General's proposal and endorsement of various repressive measures unknown either to Anglo-Saxon jurisprudence or to our own traditional legal safeguards. Early in 1970, Mr. Mitchell—a garrulous counterbalance for the "silent majority"—proposed the authorization of forced finger-printing, palm printing, physical measurements, the taking of blood, saliva and hair, and urine samples from persons suspected in one degree or another, for one cause or another, of possible criminal intent or activity. In practice if not in principle the police could presumably put out a dragnet of whatever size and haul in as many as they might be inclined to want to suspect.

Of course, it is generally assumed by those who applaud the repressive proposals of the Attorney General that such outrages would be directed to others, to "them." "Them," one assumes, has reference to the impoverished and dispossessed in our urban ghettos. Indeed, I suspect that this *is* the intent of the proposal. But one wonders what these self-righteous missionaries of "law and order" would think if, on a Sunday morning after the customary Saturday night blow-out at the local country club, all the members of the club were hauled down to the police station to undergo such outrageous treatment because a crime had been committed on the club's premises. The calloused minority—"us" rather than "them"—never imagine their own folk and friends being the victims of such abusive laws.

It is this same calloused minority which has put into currency, as though it were a respectable juridic notion, the newspeak phrase, "preventive detention." Again, the victims of this legal response to the passions of the moment would be "them," never "us." "Preventive detention" is one of the most vicious police-state tactics thus far suggested for our free democracy. Even without the abuse to which all such legislation is inevitably subject, anyone accused of a crime, or even imagined to be accusable, might be locked up without any semblance of trial procedure.

Twentieth-century Washington is not seventeenth-century Versailles, nor is Mr. Mitchell Cardinal Richelieu, however much his espousal of *lettres de cachet* makes him appear as such. Such practices as "preventive detention" are not only alien to our written laws and constitution, they are an insult to the very spirit of this democracy. As an attorney, as *the* "Attorney General," Mr. Mitchell should realize that suspension of the writ of *habeas corpus* can be undertaken only under the gravest of emergency conditions when the courts are not open and functioning. It should certainly not be undertaken at the behest of a calloused though privileged minority. Here, too, I would take my stand in the Populist tradition with Bryan:

> "I protest against the arrogant and impudent assumption that it is the privilege of any particular class to make laws for our people, or that any of our citizens, wherever their residence or whatever their occupation, are excluded from an equal voice in the affairs of government."

It has been the dubious achievement of Vice-President Agnew to have advocated exactly what Bryan excoriated. Mr. Agnew has told the nation that he strongly favors "constitutional dissent." But, improving on both Jefferson and Justice Holmes, he is very precise about its limits. Quite obviously these limits have been exceeded when elected representatives of the people ask impudent questions, or when television commentators, who have not even been elected to their jobs, respond to a Presidential speech with critical analysis instead of rhapsodies of praise. Going on to make one of those "fine distinctions" in which he specializes, the Vice-President pointed out that when the purpose of the dissent is "unsound," or when it is, in his view, "idiotic" as well, the limit of toleration has been reached. Here a milestone in jurisprudence has surely been reached, the drawing at last of a clear distinction between "constitutional" and "idiotic" dissent.

As a legal and political philosopher, the Vice-President has illustrated for each of us—if only we would listen—the kind of "subtlety" and "fine distinctions based on acute reasoning" which we, too, could perhaps make if we would stick to the text of statements, listen respectfully to the teachings of our leaders, and stop asking impudent questions about morality, the priority of values, and the national interest. Such things as these, after all, are best left to wiser heads—to such wise and venerable men as the Vice-President of the United States and to those who have made such a stunning success of American foreign policy in this decade. Or, better still, as the Vice-President himself has put it: "Saying that the President should understand the people's view is no solution. It is time for the people to understand the views of the President they elected to lead them."

But elected representatives of the people are concerned with the drift of things, with seeming misdirection and, perhaps, a warped sense of values. Some of them, undoubtedly in the mundane process of getting elected, have let their heads get filled with a lot of questions about social justice, about fairness in taxes, about peace, and about the sanctity of human life. They are so literal-minded, these impertinent demagogues! In their innocence and naïveté, they talk as though that propaganda they picked up from the people, to say nothing of Jefferson, Lincoln, and Jackson, were good for something more than inscriptions on stone monuments. Somehow they have got it in their heads that all those fine phrases, even the Bill of Rights in our Constitution, were to be taken seriously, perhaps even put into practice.

And how have our young people become infected with such "idiotic" constitutional radicalism? How have we, their parents and teachers, failed them? Mr. Agnew has an explanation and it must give us pause. "Parental-type power must be exercised," he points out. "Some parents have forgotten how." As a result of misguided permissiveness our children have fallen under the spell of "political hustlers." They do not seem to have understood—they do not seem capable of understanding—that one must attain a certain age and eminence before one has earned the right to corrupt one's country's institutions. Clearly, the Vice-President suggests, "it is time to question the credentials" of these Americans, and, perhaps, to "separate them from our society." We separated our Japanese fellow-citizens from our society during World War II, it will be recalled.

None of this is meant to suggest that the Vice-President is opposed to dissent as long as it is "constitutional," as long as it is not "unsound" or "idiotic" and as long as it does not involve criticism of the President's policies and speeches until the people have time to "digest" them, or does not involve tax policies that are fair to all of our people.

In his short tenure as President of the Senate the Vice-President has become a teacher and an example of sorts for all Senators. He warns us against ideological eunuchry; he urges us to "divide on authentic lines," and he, himself, has made an unparalleled contribution to this end. When in this era of "cool" disdain and sly innuendo have we heard such Ciceronian rhetoric as that of the Vice-President as he thunders fulminations against "vultures who sit in the trees and watch lions battle," plotting from their treetops to "pervert honest concern into something sick and rancid"? Who can hear such burning words without a stirring of the blood, without feeling inspired to sally forth against those "sick and rancid vultures" in our midst. "Their names!" we are moved to cry out.

Distressing though many aspects of it may have been, there is much to be proud of in the debate we have held among ourselves over the war in Vietnam and over the re-ordering of national priorities. It is a mark of the strength and resiliency of American democracy that we do not fear to air our differences in the open. The leaders of the Soviet Union would never dare to permit a public debate like that which we have sanctioned in recent years: they lack the necessary confidence in themselves and in their society. Perhaps Vice-President Agnew, fearing what he describes as the "whole damn zoo" of dissenters, would feel less frightened in a graveyard atmosphere where there are no dissenters. For my part, I will take a "zoo" of freedom of speech and press over a cemetery of silence and censure anytime. And so, I believe, would most Americans, because, with Justice Holmes—but not with Mr. Agnew—we know "the ultimate good desired is better reached by free trade in ideas—that the best test of truth is the power of thought to get itself accepted in the competition of the market."

What the Vice-President seems unable to realize is that the country doesn't need greater divisiveness, more inflammatory rhetoric; it doesn't need the suppression of dissent by intimidation or by law-enforcers' superior violence. It needs, instead, leadership with enlightened conscience.

In days of rapidly changing social, economic, ethnic, and political patterns, we cannot afford to preserve or rebuild our social institutions to conform to the dictates of a few or to the passions of the moment. Now if ever is the time for a calm reassessment of values and rational reconsideration of national goals. This reconstruction of our country from within calls for guidance by men who live neither in the memories of the past nor in the emotions of the present; it calls for guidance by men who are pre-eminently thinkers, men who, let it be said very simply, are concerned with a future-oriented understanding of things—it calls for guidance, if you will, by the intellectuals who over the years have voiced many of the latent convictions and beliefs of the poor and the downtrodden.

In contrast to the technocratic manipulators who have a vested interest in preserving the status quo, and the doctrinaire militants who demand change on their terms only, the authentic intellectuals of the nation, whether in the universities or the professions, have been guided less by selfish motivation or political bias and more by reasoned analysis than their counterparts in industry and government or in the revolutionary cadres of the left and right. It is the intellectuals who have preserved the inarticulate aspiration of all the people to be guided by "the rule of reason." And I personally have been pleased by the rapport I have had with the academic community, and the support it has given to the legislation and hearings I have sponsored and fostered. I am filled with revulsion at the efforts which have been made to defame, almost as a body, these men. Again, with Bryan: I do not "fear a Robespierre," I "fear a plutocracy of organized wealth and power," for instance now, a plutocracy made up of the minions of the military-industrial complex.

How can we do other than look to the wisdom of the intellectuals when our very political institutions were established during a period when leadership was exercised by intellectuals—by Jefferson, Hamilton, Madison, and the two Adamses? I have never thought they did anything other than build well, a building process we must carry on by the same lights that guided them. We cannot do this successfully under the leadership of our latter-day know-nothings. We have seen already the conseqences of following the dim lights of the anti-intellectuals: social repression, negation of civil liberties, authoritarianism—and the snobbish arrogance that always accompanies power separated from the rule of reason. Let it be said once again, and over and over, that we can and must meet the challenge of crime and violence and disorder, but we can only meet it within the framework of the intelligent exercise of human freedom.

The public, particularly the young, the idealistic, and the concerned, cannot for long be deceived. They dislike nothing so much as phoniness, such as the phoniness which masks selective repression under the badge of "law and order." Though it is said of the present generation of young people that they are overly emotional, subjective, nonrational, I do not believe this is so. They want rational solutions, but solutions that are *humanly* rational, not the kind of mechanical rationalism which views the unemployed as only a percentage point on a graph, not the chilly rationalism that computes the maimed, dead casualties of war in terms of "body count." Such people, the young, the idealistic, the concerned, who constitute the vocal majority that has spoken out for peace in two elections, want neither to wallow in sloppy sentimentality, whether chauvinistic or revolutionary, nor to abdicate their humanity in the name of a cybernetic rationalism (the Pentagon's "buttons"); they want merely to exercise their bodies and their minds, their emotions and their intelligences in, so to speak, a "sweet reasonableness." In brief, they want to act with honest intelligence and to see honest intelligence in action.

Hence, their contempt for sham, for fakery and sloganeering. And hence, too, their growing bitterness with the patently deceptive "Vietnamization" ploy. Settling the war in Vietnam merely by getting it off the front page through a verbal ruse will not now satisfy the young, the idealistic, and the concerned in America. Too many unanswered questions have been raised about the basic probity of the policies, the values, and the wisdom of our leaders. Decaying institutions have been called into question. Such icons once broken cannot be mended.

What the young in particular are questioning is our own view of ourselves. They are scrutinizing those parts of our legal and social system which do in fact lend credence to class division among us. Given their passion and their intelligence, the nation—as I have emphasized earlier—no longer has the right to withhold from them the franchise. To lower the voting age to 18 years may be a small step, but it is an important step in healing their sense of alienation and in grounding their uprootedness. How can they not but be embittered at the fakery and deception of a political system which makes them bear society's cruelest burdens while allowing them no responsible voice in its government?

There is no doubt in my mind that, when the lowering of the voting age to 18 years becomes effective, we shall see a change in public opinion on the war in Vietnam. Concomitantly, we will see a radical change in the nation's appreciation of values and a new sense of national priorities. For the one single, underlying cause of current unrest and disorder—transcending, though linked to, the integration of the Negro fully into the mainstream of American life and the poverty of great masses of our society—remains this war which was undertaken by stealth, without public knowledge and support, and without the legal underpinning to give it public sanction. If we can honorably solve the Vietnam problem, the preservation of order in our society can be left to the ordinary, constitutionally sanctioned instruments of government. We will need no phoney abrasive rhetoric or divisive crusades.

To strike out at violence in an effort to stifle dissent without analyzing the causes of violence is to sell our country short. It displays a lack of faith in the country's deeply rooted moral and spiritual reserves; and in its ability to withstand political and social stress. If the fabric of our society is strong enough, tensile enough, and anchored in its foundational documents, it can take both assault and battery—and come out stronger and healthier. If every attack sets us quaking and finds us ready to call out the shock troops, we are but running from the storm and revealing ourselves as afraid to explore the causes behind the assaults.

In earlier periods of our history it has been relatively easy to appraise the causes behind the discontent. Many have been economic, the lack of economic justice. Some of them still are and always will be, because in a free society based upon equality of opportunity, there will always be elements seeking to monopolize the nation's opportunities and resources for themselves. During all of my political life I have struck out against the privileges and sanctuaries of vested interests, and there is no evidence that this will cease to be a struggle worth engaging in.

But today's discontent is ever so much broader than merely the perennial contest of rich and poor. In the army of dissidents today march the rich and the poor, the old and the young, white and black, the cynics and the idealists, militants and pacifists; all appear to be bound together only by a common disillusionment over the gulf between the promise and the reality of American society. They have the right to despair, but their despair vests in them no new rights.

In other times, identification of the culprit was easier. Lincoln summed up the great truth in his words that a society half-slave, half-free is doomed. Wilson's resounding phrases about "a world free for democracy" and Franklin D. Roosevelt's dictum, "The only thing we have to fear is fear itself," epitomized their eras. But today there is no one phrase, no one group, no one enemy, to be singled out. The problems are multi-faceted and of many dimensions, and therefore all the more impatient of simplistic solutions. It is quite easy to blame the students—and many do—for their assaults against the Establishment. It is quite easy to blame the older generation—and many do—for their failures and their materialism. It is easy to blame all militants—and many do—for the violence and disruption which strike innocent and guilty alike. It is quite easy to blame any number of things, but how does one deal with radical disillusionment: the alien grain now flourishing in our midst? Americans, brought up on happy endings—and still devouring them nightly on television—are novices in this area. When they read, as they do today, statements to the effect that technology and bigness "have stripped life of both warmth and meaning," their first reaction is apt to be like that of Henny Penny in the old nursery story who felt that the acorn which dropped on her head was the sky falling—and rushed off with entourage to picket the king with disaster slogans.

It is incumbent upon all of us to ponder the causes of current disillusionment and move to correct as many of them as we can. We all know that violence is the antithesis of reason, whether used to coerce or to destroy. We also know that eruptions and explosions are not always the work of evildoers. Justice too long denied will eventually explode.

When in the eye of the storm, one does not call out storm troopers; one moves into a place of safe refuge, one prepares for the days ahead, and improves the instrument of forecasting and avoiding future assaults. Storms we may ever have, but we need not be their victims.

Epilogue: The Making of a Senator

To find myself labelled "Target No. 1" in that great crusade which became known as the Southern Strategy was an honor to which I certainly never aspired, but had bestowed upon me quite suddenly.

I was laboring on the floor of the U.S. Senate, my main field of operation for 18 years, using the best parliamentary skills I knew to raise the personal Income Tax exemption of each taxpayer and dependent from $600 to $1000, and hoping also to introduce other beneficial proposals into the new tax bill, when like a gauntlet thrown in the tournaments of old, I was attacked by no less an embodiment of chivalry than the Vice-President himself.

He was terribly put out with me personally, it appeared, when it became evident that the Congress intended to assert itself on what went into the tax bill, and not just endorse all the schemes for stopping inflation and placating the rich then emanating from the White House. Since tax legislation is clearly and constitutionally a prerogative of the Congress, such an attack—in the pre-Agnew era—would have been almost unthinkable. I, in all modesty, could attribute it only to the relatively solid reputation I had established through years of work in studying our tax structure and in learning the rules of the U.S. Senate. To have Vice-President Agnew recognize this was flattering indeed, but I deserved little credit for it, really, because when I first came to Washington my goal was merely to follow in the footsteps of Cordell Hull, who as a new Congressman had decided to specialize in "revenue, tariff, and other forms of taxation, economics, and finance." "I noticed," he said, "that few were interested in those subjects, but I find their dry statistics as interesting as a dime novel." I cannot go that far, nor for that matter can I imagine Mr. Hull ever reading a dime novel, but I have found the strategies of tax legislation and procedures for strengthening the national economy profoundly interesting. I only regret that I could not have achieved more in these areas than I have.

But I cast only one vote among 100 in the Senate, among 535 in the whole Congress. Thus Mr. Agnew's attack was doubly flattering. But that this one vote, entrusted to me by the people of Tennessee, is my proudest badge of achievement is no secret, and, I am not displeased to note, that it is a generally well-established fact that always to the best of my knowledge and experience, I cast it in behalf of the interests of my state and of the country in general—and this, regardless of which political party happens to control the White House. That this activity on the part of a single Senator may sometimes appear to be merely tilting at windmills is probably undeniable; though, on the other hand, if my votes receive such distinguished attention as they have from the Vice-President, perhaps the ideal of participatory democracy which I have outlined throughout this book may not be an impossible dream after all.

It is true, of course, that in recent years there has developed among the members of the Executive branch the theory that they constitute the driving force of the government, and therefore should, as it were, "own" the Legislative branch as well. A mere third of the power vested in the federal government, along with all the appointive power and most of the national budget, no longer seems to be enough for these aggrandizers of the Executive. As for the time-honored system of "checks and balances," or the traditional concept that the Executive proposes and the Legislative disposes—all this can seemingly be dispensed with. The assumption is: "Who needs it!" Well, the country and the public need it, and perhaps now more than any other time in our history when the principles of dissent and the rights of civil liberties are being encroached upon, and the poor are subjected to systematic neglect—whether "benign" or otherwise—by the Executive branch.

But let us continue to assay the recent history of Mr. Agnew, chief spokesman of unpleasantries from the Executive branch as they pertain to Congress. He coupled his flattering challenge to me with the promise that he would go to my state and campaign against my re-election. For such promised public service I expressed gratitude, and assured him there is nothing the voters of Tennessee appreciate more than having distinguished outsiders come in and instruct them on how to vote. And remembering "Br'er Rabbit" and the Tar-Baby, I thought *he* might learn a lesson in the "right to dissent."

As we have noted earlier, he generously admits that dissent is not always totally evil; it may even be permissible, he says, when it is not "idiotic" or "unsound," or does not involve criticism of the President's policies and speeches until the public has had time to "digest them"—or, we may add, does not involve tax policies for the people. The source of Mr. Agnew's befuddlement—if one believes in his sincerity, and I to an extent do—is that he bunches all dissent together and is unable (or conceivably unwilling) to distinguish between the legitimate and the disruptive. If he is *unwilling*, perhaps what I have written elsewhere in this book may instruct him; if however he is *unable*, we may be in greater peril than the Vice-President's antics suggest. For, as opined in "Coco": "A sinner can reform, but stupid is forever."

So, let us inquire just what is the Southern Strategy of which Mr. Agnew is, if not the prime tactician, at least the vocal spearhead, and how does this strategy involve me, the senior Senator from a border-state in which the electorate by preference and long tradition do their own thinking and voting? Is it real or just a figment of the press, as even many concerned officials in the Executive branch would like to have us believe? Naturally, I have no private details of this secret battle plan, but, in my opinion, it is quite "real" —although probably incorrectly labelled. It is guerilla in nature, and less "Southern" than attitudinal, being based on the assumption that all people have deep-seated prejudices which in times of social unrest can be counted upon to outweigh their sober judgment. It entails, among other things, a general purge of Congress, and uses the South as the opening wedge only because that area— unhappily too often selected to be the guinea pig for "corrective" ideas— is in the throes of an integration and public-schools crisis, and also is the base of Governor Wallace's American Party: an apparatus which the Strategy seeks to mold to its own purposes.

For me *not* to face up to the reality of this program would indicate a naïveté I can hardly be guilty of, and also an unawareness of the inflated powers which have accrued, through the years of international crises and wars, to the Executive branch. Moreover, it would indicate an igorance of what great wealth can at times accomplish in the political order.

The Strategy, whatever its geographic or prejudicial perimeters, has placed me in the eye of a storm, and from where I stand in 1970 the gales and driving rains are both evident and destructive. I know it is not raining pennies from heaven for me out there, but dollars for my opposition, and that the real name of this storm is simply "purge politics"—*Carthago delenda est!* So *The Eye of the Storm* is the title I have chosen for this book, a storm which is raging across the nation, but which I see as focused upon my own state of Tennessee. In the face of this storm, my only protective resort is my record—including not only my votes, but my beliefs and dreams about democracy, and my eagerness to fight for my views on some of the issues critical to America in our time.

In these chapters I have tried both to cover the highlights of my Congressional career, and also to outline a viable American politics for the future. In this concluding epilogue, I can perhaps be more informal, and try to "explain" myself to the reader—as if anyone, let alone a person in public life, ever could adequately explain the multifarious paths and the infinity of influences which have led him to his present conclusions.

The Senate is not a club as so often said, but an arena filled with 99 strong-willed, independent, egotistical, and scrappy men—and one woman possessed of those same general traits. For better or worse, these qualities are the ingredients of national decision-making, and of what a recent President termed the political consensus in this diverse country. The element of ego stems partly from pride in the states which elected them and imparts a courage which might not be inborn, but which is a natural (and helpful) trait in most politicians. A single Senator can but rarely tip the scales very far, and this is all to the good: the cult of the infallible and unquestioned leader has no place in our form of government.

What a lone Senator can do is stand by his principles, do his homework, know his people, attend to his committee meetings, and be prepared for his afternoons in the arena. What he says and does there, his votes that day, may possibly be decisive in favor of legislation which he advocates. But it may be just as important to vote against a bad bill, even if he knows it is going to pass, simply in order to register his dissent. He cannot possibly become an expert in everything which comes before the Senate, but if he develops a broad knowledge of a few basic areas, he will almost inevitably have also cultivated, by this very process, a political and moral philosophy which will guide his action in others.

In brief, he must be willing to face the storm, even to cope with "the eye of the storm." Our beliefs, our ethics, our hopes for the future are now all storm-wracked, assailed from the Right, and the New Right, the Left, and the New Left. Incidentally, those are terms I deplore just as I look askance at those who apply such facile and indiscriminate tags as bourgeoisie, proletariat, Communist-sympathizer, the little man, the silent majority, the quasi-liberal, etc. Several tags, though so far as I know none of the above, have been attached to me during my political career. One of these is "maverick," and if one likes labels, this in some ways may be an apt description. It is apt in the sense that most Tennesseans are mavericks, since they are opposed to running thoughtlessly with the herd, feel no need to play follow the leader, and value their personal and social independence. For this reason, only someone who is a maverick, not out of the desire to build a political image, but out of principle, can truly represent such a state.

In this long and narrow Sixteenth State into the union, the second west of the Alleghenies—stretching laterally and literally from the Smokies to the Mississippi—can be found almost all types of climate, vegetation, scenery, *and* voters: all different. We have, as no other states do, an east, a middle, and a west, each section of which is distinctive. It would be extremely unlikely if all the citizens of such a geographically and culturally different locale were to agree unanimousy on a single subject—and I cannot recall that it ever has happened. Apparently the nearest the people of this state came to total unanimity was back in the Mexican War days when the call went out for 2600 soldiers and 30,000 volunteers answered it, from which event it derives the title "Volunteer State."

It is not that Tennesseans are "contrary" by nature, but that their long and pronounced pioneer heritage and their diverse backgrounds have developed in them an individuality which no amount of industrialization seems to lessen; for those same reasons, during most of their history they have been blessedly immune to demagoguery and political sloganeering.

Whenever reflecting on my political career, I inevitably recall the humid day in September, 1938, when my wife and I first arrived in Washington together. I had no appointments there, no business to transact, in fact no real purpose for going, except that I had just been nominated to the Congressional Seat from the Fourth District of Tennessee, and simply could not wait to look the place over. My nomination was tantamount to election and I was enflamed by the desire to get down to work; my head was swimming with things I wished to do for the people of my new district. With all the confidence of youth, I was certain that this would be the scene of notable, perhaps even noble, exploits as I fulfilled my childhood ambition.

That ambition may have started during my first week in a one-room schoolhouse in a mountain cove some 50 miles east of Nashville, a city I would not see for several years. I know that a small fire was lit, perhaps not a political one, when my first teacher, Miss Mary Litchford, had me stand up before the entire school body because I had learned the alphabet in just one week. When a little later a cousin ran for the state legislature and had his picture on utility poles and roadside trees, in my childish imagination I was fascinated by the prospect of seeing my own picture there some day. However, during modest "commencement exercises" at the school, I developed a new passion which temporarily detoured my incipient political ambitions. Because I had a verse to recite, I was seated near the stage where the musicians were, and I became utterly entranced by my first taste of country music—especially that of the fiddle.

The fiddler was known to everyone as Uncle Berry Agee, and as our elders said, "He sure drew a wicked bow." As he would cut down on "Turkey in the Straw," "Arkansas Traveller," and "Old Joe Clark," the crowded schoolroom would rock with rhythm while people stamped their feet and clapped their hands. When he would change his pace to an old waltz like "Over the Waves," the mood grew quieter.

That night I asked my mother to buy me a fiddle—she was the one who did things like that for us children. My father's earnings went into mortgage payments on the farm, fence mending and barn fixing—and small savings. Personal spending money came from the sale of butter, eggs, chickens, turkeys, black walnuts, and from winter trappings. My mother did not know where to buy a fiddle, but thought there might be one in a pawnshop in Nashville; and as I kept up my nagging, when my brother, twelve years older than I, went with a local trucker to take some livestock to market, mother gave him $5 to find me a fiddle. He made a deal for $4, and the fiddle was mine. I recall how sad and disappointed I was when I drew the bow, and what came forth did not sound at all like Uncle Berry. The only man in the neighborhood who knew about tuning and playing lived some distance away, so after the day's work and supper, I trudged to his house, and night after night followed his instructions. Very generously, as I can realize now, he said I had "a natural ear" for music, and soon I was laboriously, but happily, sawing out "Old Joe Clark." I played it incessantly much to the distress of my family who were equally embarrassed when I subjected every visitor who happened by to the same melody over and over. Finally my father said, "Son, if you can't learn another tune you'd better quit."

So over to Uncle Berry Agee's I went one weekend, to see if I could learn "Turkey in the Straw." By now I was back in school, and with after-school chores could not get to practicing until after supper, all of which interfered with my father's early-to-bed, early-to-rise schedule. After a while he suggested, very gently, that there was a huge limestone boulder nearby and under it a fox den, and that the foxes, being nocturnal in habit, just might enjoy my music. So on moonlit nights, to the boulder I would go, and by the time I finished eighth grade, I was regarded as a fairly good fiddler. In fact, my interest in music had become all-absorbing, and I was accepted by other musicians and permitted to play at square dances. (Years later I learned to tolerate my own son's interest in rock music by recalling my father's patience with me.)

Had it not been for my father, I probably never would

have renewed my interest in politics. He imparted his final lesson after a hoe-down at our house to which all the neighbors and several musicians were invited. Among the latter was the best mandolin picker of the whole area: "Old Peg," he was called. He was helpful and patient with me, and the sharp notes of his mandolin harmonized well with the fiddle. He was the first to arrive for the hoe-down in his ramshackle buggy drawn by a mangy horse, with his mandolin carefully wrapped like the treasure it was to him. It was a wonderful hoe-down! My mother, happy to have so much company, remarked that she was glad she had bought the fiddle, and my father seemed to enjoy himself more than I'd ever noticed him doing before. Old Peg spent the night, and next morning after one of my mother's lavish breakfasts—fried chicken, ham, eggs, preserves, fried corn, and hot biscuits—my father and I helped hitch his horse and buggy. His harness was tied together with baling wire and binder twine; the buggy was without a top, and one wondered how long the wheels would stay on. When he was out of hearing range, wheels wobbling down the road, my father—his hand on my shoulder—said in words that I will never forget: "Son, there goes your future."

This quiet and understated admonition shocked me as few things in my life have. I entered high school the next week determined to learn more than "Turkey in the Straw." After graduation three years later and a short course in teacher training, I went to teach in Overton County at a school which Uncle Charlie Gore, a member of the school board, had me assigned to in a little Cumberland Mountain community named High Land—but known as "Booze" since it was an active manufacturing center for moonshine. It was impossible to get to Booze by car, so Uncle Charlie drove me to the foot of the mountain and I set out—with my fiddle and parcel of clothing and books—to walk the last five miles. At a fork in the path there was no sign to guide me, so I rested and fiddled until a stranger approached. "You are the new teacher, aren't you?" he asked after I had introduced myself and inquired about the way to Booze. "I'm going to meetin' there so we can walk together."

Booze was a beautiful little place, its eight houses scattered underneath huge beech trees along each side of a ravine. There was a general store and an old grist mill with a big wooden water wheel—and the one-room schoolhouse which was also used for religious services. A revival was under way that Sunday morning and my new friend, after introducing me to a few people, asked me to sit on the stage and join the choir.

The leader of the choir was Ernest Ledbetter, who coached the singing which—surprisingly—was really excellent. Three country boys with immense undulating adams' apples were letting out with a wonderful bass, and a lovely brown-eyed girl named Orpha, Ernest's sister, was singing alto—though I must confess more than her voice caught my attention. I joined the tenors, but they were quite beyond me and, as they sang by notes, I did not do very well. After the hymns, the preacher opened the service by calling upon "Professor Gore" to talk. Well, the Professor was 18 years of age, and though he had all of three months of college behind him he had never previously been called upon to speak before a group. And the results were as one might have expected.

This dismal debut was partially redeemed the next morning when at 8 o'clock instead of the expected 25 students, more than 40 came—including Orpha and several friends who had their curiosity piqued by the new professor. Her presence raised something of a problem for me and gave me my first lesson in private interest versus public interest; I think I managed to put the public interest first, though I'm afraid my private interest in Orpha survived.

This was my "Appalachian Spring," and during it I learned to appreciate the virtues of the Tennessean, virtues which have stood unchanged from the days of Andrew Jackson to those of Cordell Hull, and which are still honored to this day.

I boarded with the family of Arkley Gore, who lived near the school. We could never prove any kinship but probably were cousins, because it was to this country that my ancestors had come with a land grant for services in the Revolution. Arkley Gore's home had two rooms and a lean-to, but there was space for me because they had only one child, and also because they needed the board money, which was $1 a day from my salary of $75 a month. Arkley Gore worked in a coal mine five miles over the mountain, leaving on muleback by daybreak and returning late and tired: black with coal dust, his eyes nevertheless clear and full of love for his wife and daughter. The hardship of this life was driven home to me in many ways, but especially by the meals we were served. Only once in the four months I was there did we have meat, other than on those occasions when I brought it back from my afternoons of hunting: a sport in which I delighted. In addition to roaming the mountains with a rifle, I enjoyed Ernest Ledbetter's singing class, where, with Orpha's aid, I learned to read what we called "shape notes," and to follow a tuning fork in singing either bass or tenor.

By Christmas I had $200 with which to enter the University of Tennessee for the January term. I was most anxious by then to obtain a college degree and study law with a view to entering politics. At the University I waited tables in a downtown restaurant for my meals, but even with this and other economies, I realized I would never have enough money to continue my program. My experiences were typical of the times, and I hoped that from a summer in Detroit—a source of income for many poor Tennesseans—I would be able to save enough money for one continuous year of schooling. My father warned against this move after having read in *The Nashville Banner* about the growing unemployment in the north. "If you don't get a job I'll have to send you money to come home on," he said. But a schoolmate and I decided to risk it. Though we had luck with our hitchhiking, we had none whatever with jobs, and spent day after day standing in lines before employment windows. One temporary job to help build a new telephone line was all I obtained until, through a private agency, I heard of a farmer who needed help. By then I had exactly 33 cents left and used it to ride the streetcar as far north as it went, and walked the remaining distance. I milked 12 cows night and morning and pitched hay during the day. The summer was a financial disaster, but I arrived home proud that my father had not been obliged to send me money. Remorsefully I had to admit to him, "I would have been better off to have stayed home and helped you."

During that summer I pondered upon my own happy childhood and wondered why it had been so. I concluded it was because we lived apart from the world, relatively isolated and therefore dependent entirely upon one another. Although the chores were heavy and the discipline absolute, there was love in our family and reverence for each other. Probably few young people of today would understand that discipline, and I wouldn't want to glorify or exaggerate its merits, but we did live in a self-giving, self-respecting household, and that household certainly had a head.

I was fortunate enough that autumn to teach in a one-room scoolhouse on Little Creek in my own county at a salary of $85 a month, $35 of which went for board. The family I lived with had a four-room frame whitewashed house and a visibly better standard of living, which I attributed to the income from a small veteran's pension, an occasional day's work as a substitute rural mail carrier, and a small amount of creek bottom land to farm. Arkley Gore had had no land except a rough and unproductive hillside.

Again, I returned to college in January and the next September was promoted to principal of a 3-teacher school. "Professor Gore" was making it! I even delivered my first political speech by introducing a Congressman when the campaign between Al Smith and Herbert Hoover was under way. Although not yet old enough to vote, I was zealously opposed to Hoover. In 1933 I finished college and ran for County Superintendent of Schools against a man whose distinguished career had nevertheless (as happens in politics) engendered considerable opposition. It was a strenuous door-to-door campaign which I seemed to be winning—until the absentee votes were counted. My opponent had both the funds and foresight to send campaigners to Detroit, Akron, and Toledo to obtain absentee ballots totaling 300 which more than wiped out my 182-vote majority. This was the only election I have ever lost. It was also my first initiation into the value of organization and the role of money in our political life.

Local politics being what they were (and still are), having challenged and lost, there was no teaching job for me. So I returned to my father's farm and, as we said, "made a crop," working in the fields and woods for a whole year to produce a net income of exactly $89 and some cents. The inequity of this had a lasting influence on me. I could live on this pittance because my father had paid off his mortgage and I was staying at home. But as I looked around that day at the marketplace and saw men with wives and children whom they could neither feed nor clothe well and whose farms were not paid for, I recognized the face of poverty: grown men who were so desperate the tears streamed down their cheeks as they stood with me at the window to receive their meager checks for a full year's work.

I vowed to remember the ignominy of their plight, and in later years was instrumental in legislating programs to benefit the small family farmer. My own condition was embarrassing for a college graduate, but never desperate—and, with the arrogance of youth, I was convinced I could improve it by simply "getting out and finding a job." I stood a week in the employment line at the DuPont rayon plant at Old Hickory near Nashville but was turned away each day without an interview. I tried to borrow $40 from a bank at Carthage, my county seat, and now my home, so I could tackle Detroit once more—but the answer was a firm "no." I finally found work driving a truck for a local furniture man at $12.50 a week—and so stumbled into my first business break.

In order to collect for the furniture, my employer thought it necessary to take in trade small batches of tobacco from the farmers. He knew nothing about tobacco, but as my father grew it, I—again quite presumptuously—thought I did. So I bought it from him, regraded it, and sold the first batch for $40 profit. By the end of the tobacco season I had several hundred dollars: the largest sum of money I had ever possessed, and in my euphoria I decided to visit Washington. My Congressman was J. Ridley Mitchell, who greeted me with great cordiality, as he did everyone who came to see him. (There was a saying in the old Fourth District that he was the only Congressman who could promise every constituent a post office and then make him happy not to get it.) I watched him and the other Congressmen from the gallery, and though I was not sure whether they were doing a good job, I had no trouble convincing myself that I could do as well.

I returned home to find that the man I had failed to unseat as County Superintendent of Schools was dying of cancer, and had recommended me to friends for his job because in my campaign I had never attacked him personally—something new in his experience. The county court elected me overwhelmingly, and I learned another fruitful political lesson: to minimize the personal angle in campaigns, and to engage in principles not in personalities.

My new job was most rewarding in that it gave me real public responsibility and an acquaintance with self-government at the local level. The political pressures in my small bailiwick were immediate and intense, but with a four-year term ahead of me, I felt free to follow night classes at the YMCA Law School in Nashville. This required driving more than a 100 miles three nights a week for three years, but was more than rewarding, and not only in terms of the education I received—for during this period I met another law student, Miss Pauline LaFon, whom I later married. She was a student at Vanderbilt Law School by day and waited tables at the nearby Andrew Jackson coffee shop at night. My consumption of coffee increased dramatically, and soon I was driving her home every night after work. Meanwhile, on the advice of Judge J. M. Gardenhire, I was accepting all speaking engagements which came my way. "You may make a poor speech," he said, "but there'll always be at least one damn fool who thought it was a good one." So the news made the rounds that Superintendent Gore was ambitioning higher office—which he assuredly was.

My first statewide contacts came when Congressman Gordon Browning ran for the U.S. Senate. I became his campaign manager and together we built a party organization which through the years remained loyal to both of us. He lost the Senate race, but two years later was elected Governor and asked me to become his Commissioner of Labor. My own depression experiences motivated me strongly, and soon we inaugurated unemployment compensation in Tennessee, against the opposition of some business interests.

The state was changing, becoming increasingly industrialized and urbanized, with ever fewer family farms and households where food was plentiful and young men could return during periods of unemployment. Remembering Arkley Gore's coal-mining experience, I took seriously my responsibility for administering the Mine Inspection Law. I was horrified to learn that the inspectors I had inherited from the previous administration made not even the least pretense of actually entering the mines to check on working conditions. It was necessary to dismiss them all, and, with the approval of the Governor, to purchase testing equipment and to hire qualified men who would report on the actual conditions. Here, too, one met with personal hostility, and the only shield one could erect against such animus was the conviction that social reforms must be carried out even if they offend the vested interests.

I was well into my second year in office when Congressman Mitchell, in a move surprising to me, declared his candidacy for the U.S. Senate. I was in my office when the news was released and when reporters began calling, I immediately announced for his seat. I resigned as Commissioner and returned temporarily to my father's farm, this time with wife and baby daughter, to prepare my speeches and improve my delivery—once again testing myself among the trees and limestone boulders. I wrote what I thought was a great speech, but the verdict from family and friends was that it lacked spontaneity and was "too high flown." I was now 29 years of age, but looked younger, and some said I was too young for a Congressional seat. To counteract this, I was advised always to wear my coat while speaking, to act with great dignity, and above all "to never play that damn fiddle because if you do you will appear as undignified as you are and your opponents will say you are fiddling while Rome burns."

I had five opponents and had to cover 18 counties with a population of 300,000. I managed to borrow $3000, and my friends raised a few hundred more; so with this my wife and I campaigned together and separately both day and night. The sum we had was meager even then, and today would be pathetically inadequate, but through the hot days I managed to keep on my coat and stay away from the fiddle—that is, until I reached Jamestown in the Cumberland Mountains. The courthouse was filled and the aisles crowded, and since it was native Cordell Hull territory, I was explaining his reciprocal trade program when, about halfway through my statistics, I saw an old fiddling friend come in, and behind him two others with guitar and banjo. They came up front and stood directly before me requesting that I play a tune with them. The audience cheered but I shook my head. Finally I saw I had no choice, so I took the fiddle and continued to talk while tuning it, telling my listeners that some people had thought I was too young for Congress, and that fiddling would further detract from my appearance. "But," I said, "all of you know I'm a fiddler—and not ashamed of it. I'll make a deal—I'll play the fiddle if you'll vote for me." The applause was resounding. I played and told stories and talked seriously for about an hour as the crowd grew larger. The entire performance was a great success, and *The Nashville Tennessean* ran a front page story about it on Sunday. Thereafter, wherever Gore went he fiddled! Eventually I took with me some of my musician neighbors, and, interspersed with "Casey Jones" and "Arkansas Traveller," I tried to discuss the problems of the people as I saw them. So, notwithstanding my youth, my lack of dignity, *and* my fiddling, I was elected by a handsome majority.

The next month when my wife and I made our unscheduled visit to Washington, I called on Vice-President John Nance Garner who welcomed me as a Congressman-elect, and offering me a glass of bourbon—which I declined—told me: "Young man, I never saw a Congressman defeated for something he didn't say and didn't do." The more I thought about this suggestion to do and say as little as possible in order to keep on being elected, the less I liked it. I also called on Secretary of State Hull who then gave me the only piece of direct advice he ever offered during our long friendship. He advised me simply to "stay on the floor and learn the rules" because they would be useful in the future.

As a freshman, I found the pace of Congressional activity frustratingly slow; as in my father's household, the youngsters were to be seen and not heard. It was two months before a committee assignment was given to me on Banking and Currency. Though not the committee of my choice, it provided valuable experience which shaped my attitude towards the kind of fiscal reform I have discussed earlier in this book. The pitfalls of the seniority system were brought home to me most embarrassingly when I sought to retain a job as Capitol policeman for a constituent. Then as now such jobs around the Capitol were parceled out by the patronage committee whose chairman at that time was Congressman Sol Bloom of New York. I went to see him and was explaining the plight of this young man, who had been going to night school while working as a policeman and lacked only one year for graduation, when he cut me off with an imperious: "How impertinent for a freshman to ask for a policeman! Impossible!" and turned away. That was all—for then.

I determined to reciprocate in kind. The World's Fair was planned for New York that year and before long Sol, as I thereafter called him, placed a resolution before Congress asking for $275,000 in federal funds for the fair. I sought out all the other freshmen in the Congress and, after narrating my story, told them that I was preparing an amendment to Sol's bill that $30,000 of it be channeled to three forthcoming events in my own district: $10,000 each for the Carthage Fair, the Lebanon Mule Day, and the Petersburg Colt Show. The scheme proved contagious and the other newcomers also began to prepare their amendments. When Sol called up his bill we were ready for him—but the Democratic leader, Sam Rayburn, advised Sol to set his resolution aside for a few days. Well, Democrats have a way of getting together; my constituent graduated in his policeman's uniform, and I attended the New York World's Fair at the personal invitation of Congressman Bloom.

On the Banking and Currency committee I favored Roosevelt's Home Owners Loan Corporation to stem the growing wave of mortgage foreclosures across the country. Though opponents produced great numbers of statistics before the committee to prove that the government would lose immense amounts of money in the venture, in fact it turned out to be a profitable undertaking. In the committee I also initiated efforts to establish farm price supports. This was an extension of an earlier proposal, right after Pearl Harbor, that the government should establish over-all wage and price controls. The President, who was the great hero of my generation, called me to the White House and, although intrigued by the idea, said that the country was not ready for it yet—though in the following year he produced his own plan for economic stabilization which included such controls. In advocating my later proposal for the farmers, I argued that it was only fair they should have floor prices supported for them, even as the workers in industry and other trades had a minimum wage. The concept of parity prices and parity income grew out of this proposal.

Also as a member of the committee I was able to witness at firsthand Roosevelt's deft handling of monetary policy during the war. The interest rates on government bonds were never allowed to exceed 2½ per cent, and the prime rate in New York banks never exceeded 2 per cent. When the new apostles of *laissez-faire* mourn the advancing interest rates and lament that there is nothing the government can do, I always cite the performance of Roosevelt, as also of Truman who during the Korean War kept rates down.

As I have mentioned earlier, my greatest frustration was being excluded from effective tax legislation. I realized the unique strength of the Senatorial office here, as well as in a number of other areas in which battles lost in the House were salvaged in the Senate. As acting chairman for the subcommittee handling funds for the Atomic Energy Commission, the Oak Ridge atomic facilities, for long a top secret, came within my jurisdiction. Detailed knowledge of the atomic program thus gained was the best preparation for my later Senate actions on the nuclear weapons test treaty, nuclear arms limitation, the ABM debate, and the conflict over nuclear power. During this entire period, I spent a great deal of time studying the various government agencies and becoming familiar with every government or government-aid program in my state—and welcomed invitations to speak at any public affairs in Tennessee. For—as one may have surmised—I wanted to move to the Senate.

Senator K. D. McKellar had announced that he would not run again, and since no other Congressman could match my availability, I decided to make the move for his seat. What I had not anticipated was that the Senator would change his mind. This upset me both personally and politically because he had been an effective Senator, and for the most part we had worked together for TVA and other projects; but I felt that I could not reverse myself at his behest. To my mind, I had burned my bridges, nor could I stand aside for the election of a Senator who at the close of his term of office would be 92 years of age. I announced, and so did he. It was an unusual campaign. I never spoke of him except in a complimentary way—though always in the past tense. The opposition printed thousands of placards saying:

Thinking feller
Vote for McKellar.

We countered with placards placed just beneath them:

Think some more
and vote for Gore.

My victory was singularly gratifying to me both because my freshman period proved to be a short one, and because several of my newly elected colleagues were former House members with whom I had served. When the Dixon-Yates contract was exposed—as I have already mentioned—I launched the fight against it with a 7-hour extemporaneous speech, which was in no sense a filibuster, but rather an elaborate effort to detail the heinousness of the proposed giveaway. I had warm support in that fight from Senators Hill and Sparkman of Alabama, Cooper of Kentucky, and my colleague Estes Kefauver; in fact, the contract was finally undone through the efforts of Senator Kefauver's investigating committee. For me personally the triumph was sweet because I had proved my mettle as a Senator on the very floor of the Senate itself.

Anxious to redeem my enforced exclusion from tax legislation in the House, I asked to be placed on the Senate Finance Committee, but was frustrated by Lyndon Johnson, then Democratic Leader of the Senate, who made it clear that from his standpoint I was wrong on oil, and told me I would have to wait a long time for a seat on the committee. (Four years, as it turned out!) He offered me another major committee, but I told him I would prefer to wait for Finance. I received Public Works, which though not a major committee, provided me with an opportunity to author the Interstate Highway Bill which initiated the largest public works program the world has ever known.

With a successful fight on the Senate floor, and a major bill to my credit, along with a few instances of attention-getting debate, I was in demand as a Party speaker at Democratic dinners and other affairs across the country. All of this was rather heady activity, and I liked it. There's a cloakroom saying on Capitol Hill: "When a Senator looks in the mirror he sees a President." In truth, that lure never really overwhelmed me, though there were times when the Vice-Presidency seemed extremely attractive. For the most part, however, I simply followed Cordell Hull's advice and "stayed on the floor and learned the rules."

During my second year in the Senate, the Supreme Court rendered its 1954 decision, Brown *v.* Board of Education, which stunned my constituency. My own first personal shock from the racial cruelty of our system of segregation came to me only when I was driving my wife and small daughter, Nancy, to Washington to begin my term as a new Congressman. With us, as a nurse for Nancy, was Mrs. Ocie Bell Hunt, a Negro. I soon discovered that it was difficult to find filling stations between Tennessee and Washington which would permit her to use a rest room. I began asking if she could use the facilities before I placed my order for gasoline. If the answer was "no," I sought another place. The food problem was easier to manage but equally humiliating. I solved it by ordering for her and taking it to her myself —to eat in the car. As for lodging, we could find no place on that first trip which would permit her to stay overnight. Later we reached an understanding with a motel owner that if we called ahead and then arrived after dark he would accommodate us. Generally, though, we set out early and made the 650-mile trip in one long, tiring day to avoid embarrassment. I have never forgotten such unbelievable cruelty.

The Court's decision outlawing segregation in the public school system evoked in my state protests and denunciations, along with demands that Congress defy or undo the law. I could not, however, bring myself to say the decision was wrong. As a former superintendent of schools, I knew the "separate but equal" schools were inferior: segregation *was* discrimination. Soon it became necessary for me to take a public stand. Strom Thurmond, then as now an activist, composed most of the document that came to be known as the "Southern Manifesto." Where or how it was so named, I never knew, but it soon became the litmus test of Southern regional loyalty. The prestigious Senator Walter George introduced it, but Thurmond was the real *agent provocateur*. It was he who presented it to me for my approval and signature. I read it once and gave him a definite, flat "no."

Much of my constituency was outraged at me. They "expected as much of Kefauver," many of them said, "but not Albert." I replied that my grandfather had tried unsuccessfully to secede from the Union in 1861, and I had no wish to emulate him in the middle of the twentieth century. No one was satisfied with this, and the furor swelled. I regarded the "manifesto" (what an irritating and pretentious name!) as the most unvarnished piece of demagoguery I had ever encountered. Moreover, I was convinced that my fellow Southerners—and that is how I regarded them—were misleading their people, and that nothing but tragedy could come of open defiance of the law. It was my sincere conviction that they were doing a disservice while I represented the enlightened and the best interests of the South. But this is not how many people saw it. I was placed in the anguishing position of either violating my legislative conscience by signing a thoroughly unsound document or of appearing to go "against the South." Extremists still launch the "anti-South" epithet at me, and my refusal to sign the "manifesto" was the principal weapon used against me in my campaign for re-election in 1958. But my faith in the good sense of the people of my state was exonerated because, although my refusal to sign lost me my membership in the Southern Senators' Club, it did not lose me my seat in the Senate. I took a stand on principle and the people of my state approved.

My service in the Congress has been during the greatest social revolution of modern times, if not the greatest peaceful revolution of all times—a revolution that would undoubtedly have continued and accelerated were it not for the abortive war in Vietnam and its attendant dislocation of national priorities. I have been in the vanguard of much of this reformatory activity. Sometimes snidely, sometimes perjoratively, more rarely praisingly, I have been called a "reformer": of this I am proud. We are in a period now when we could stand a wholesale national reformation to strengthen us and unite us to withstand the assaults of the far Right, launched by those who would capitalize on ignorance and prejudice, and of the far Left, which attacks democracy through violence and disruption.

I have occasionally been accused of voting my private convictions, and of ignoring the expressed wishes of my constituents. Nothing could be further from the truth. No politician can afford to be, and none wants to be, indifferent to the wishes of the people he represents. Moreover, if he were foolish enough to lapse into indifference, he would soon be retired; and I have not been defeated in pursuit of public office since I was first chosen superintendent of schools for Smith County at the age of 24.

Certainly, I do plead guilty to sometimes ignoring a vociferous minority, and at other times to turning a deaf ear to directives from self-proclaimed spokesmen of non-existent groups or lobbies of "thousands of voters." There is no such thing as "instant politics," but if there were some foolproof method whereby I could determine on hundreds of issues how four million Tennesseans feel and think, I would certainly employ it. Reliable information on public sentiment, even though temporary, is valuable to a representative of the people.

But I must vote when the roll is called, and I have no choice but to represent my constituents in the light of my own best judgment. Furthermore, I embrace the political philosophy of Cordell Hull, who, in recalling his elections to the House of Representatives in 1907, said: "I felt that any Congressman worth his salt should be able to furnish leadership in his district and at the same time perform a much broader duty to the nation as a whole. This duty manifestly devolves upon him and is in addition to that towards his immediate constituents." It devolves even more so on a Senator—who represents a whole state—because he is one-hundredth of the most powerful legislative group in the world. He represents his state nationally, and his vote and voice represent a segment of national responsibility.

This dual role of representing the people of Tennessee and the Nation has not often troubled me. I believe that in almost every case, if not in every case, what benefits the Nation as a whole will benefit Tennessee and its citizens, and that what stifles progress is a blind, parochial, regional loyalty. The great English parliamentarian, Edmund Burke, observed:

> "It ought to be the happiness and glory of a representative to live in strictest union, the closest correspondence, and the most unreserved communication with his constituents. Their wishes ought to have great weight with him; their opinion high respect; their business unremitted attention. It is his duty to sacrifice his repose, his pleasures, his satisfaction, to theirs; and above all, ever, and in all cases, to prefer their interests to his own.
>
> "Your representative owes you, not his industry only, but his judgment; and he betrays instead of serving you if he sacrifices it to your opinion."

A Congressman, if he believes in our three-branch form of government and in representing his constituency, cannot let himself be swayed from his duty as he sees it by always waiting to hear from home or determining what the occupant of the White House wants before making up his mind. He has the responsibility of initiation as well as of independence of thought.

In this decade of the 1970's, the storm will be upon us. It is my firm belief that the dissipation of the storm clouds, the restoration of domestic tranquility, is the first order of business; but, as I have emphasized throughout this book, this cannot be brought about until we have broken the shackles of our Vietnam commitment and have reordered our military and international obligations. My deepest fear is that totalitarian methods may move into the ascendency, and the right to legitimate dissent may be lost for a harmfully long period. This would be a bitter nostrum for the country as a whole: it would punish not only those who may deserve punishment, but would tear the whole fabric of our society into shreds, and reverse the social progress we have made in the past four decades.

Out of the jungle of technological achievement, much of it quite incomprehensible to many Americans, comes a kind of mass stupefaction which is intensified by the war in Vietnam and its concomitant evils. It may be difficult frequently to tell which way progress lies, except by a kind of negative standard: those who make their appeal to blindness, prejudice, and littleness of mind and spirit are the enemies of progress.